Life is a contest,
And when I fail to compete I will die,
And even though the grim reaper may not collect my body,
When I fail to compete I will surrender to the comfort of the bells,
And my soul will belong to my keeper,
For life is a contest.

—William G. Baker 1259-AZ

To Sean
+
Matthew

William G. Baker
Feb 18, 2017

If you want to comment on the contents of this book, your words are welcome at billbaker1259@gmail.com

All the photos in the front section of this book owe credit to the following:
The National Archives and Record Administration, International Press Photos, Image Vault, Acme Photo Service, and Michael Esslinger, author and Alcatraz historian.

Alcatraz Prison: See the cell house on top of the hill, factory building along the waterfront.

Forest Tucker, bank-robber and leader of the Alcatraz band. A great guy, he was to become a lifetime friend.

The wide corridor between B and C blocks called Broadway.

Warden Paul Madigan ("Promising Paul") with convict Blackie Audett, behind, in whites and bow tie.

ISBN-13: 978-1482754070
ISBN-10: 148275407X
BISAC: Biography & Autobiography / Criminals & Outlaws

Every word in this book is true to the best of my memory of events and conversations that took place while I was serving time at Alcatraz and that I witnessed with my own eyes and heard with my own ears and felt with my own heart. As I write this I am eighty years old, and while today I may forget where I put my false teeth last night, like many old men I have a clear and vivid memory of events and conversations that happened in my youth many, many years ago. This is the true account of that time in my life when I was a bad boy.

Warning—strong language in character with a prison environment. This account is told from the viewpoint of the Alcatraz convict.

—William G. Baker 1259-AZ

Alcatraz Cell (dressed up for show). Cells were only 5′ x 9′

Mess Hall, 1962. They believed in feeding good at Alcatraz. They had no canteen, so you couldn't buy any snacks, so you couldn't miss any meals, which I didn't.

To Mae

When God made Mae He must have dipped her in honey, because she is the sweetest woman in the world.

Recreation Yard, 1956. Daytime rec weekends & holidays only.

D Block — the "hole" (six punishment cells bottom tier, back)

Richard (Jackrabbit) Bayless, bank-robber. A quiet and thoughtful man, he too was to become a lifetime friend.

Aaron Burget. He died trying to escape. They found his body floating in the Bay but his soul was long gone.

FOREWORD

Hello.

I'm Bill Baker. I guess I'm one of the last living prisoners from Alcatraz, that's what I've been told. I know that everybody I knew from Alcatraz is dead, gone to that big prison in the sky, for I know that the Bureau of Prisons must have figured out a way to build a prison there and that Federal Prison Industries has built a factory there to employ the heavenly convicts, for they don't miss a chance. I once heard that if you die at Alcatraz they bury your body standing up and don't lay it down until your time is up, but I think it's more likely that you go straight up, or maybe straight down, and finish your time sewing white cotton gloves for Federal Prison Industries.

I'm retired now. I've been trying to retire for many years, and I finally got a parole officer who was wise enough to let me. They don't really need me anymore anyway, for there are millions of young gang-bangers and crack-heads and such out there just knocking on prison doors to get in, enough to provide job security for the entire criminal justice system for ever and ever, so why bother with me. The gang-bangers are easier to catch anyway. They shoot each other, and the ones who get shot go to the hospital and the ones who survive run to their mama's house.

I retired at the top of my game. I'm the best counterfeit check casher there is. I learned my trade at Alcatraz from Courtney Taylor, the best there was. The only problem is the best isn't good enough. You can get away with it a thousand times, but all you have to do is get caught once and you're caught.

I guess you could say I'm a career criminal, but that really doesn't fit my track record, for a career criminal jacket best fits somebody with a greater degree of success than I had. You could better describe me as a career convict. I mean I've either been a convict or an ex-convict all my life, doing a life sentence on the installment plan. But, for all that, I'm still the best there is. I just can't seem to solve the problem of getting caught.

Not that the law is so smart. They never once caught me by their own effort. They didn't have to. I caught myself, one little mistake after another, on the job training, but that's what it takes to be the best, I guess.

I have no love for the law, nor they for me, but me and the law had a congenial dumb and dumber relationship, they being dumb and me being dumber.

Now at eighty years of age they've turned me out to pasture. It's nice to not be needed any more. Once upon a time, though, I was desperately needed. The Bureau of Prisons needed me to fill up a bed. The Federal Prison Industries needed me to work in their factories. And when I was free, every cop from sea to shining sea wanted me badly, had a set of shiny handcuffs ready just for me. I can imagine law enforcement agencies throughout the land saying, "Oh shit! Baker's on the loose again!" For I was wide open and they knew me well by name. So there were a lot of "Oh shits" when I was free.

Now I'm a relic, a fossil from a time before the gang-bangers came along and changed the world with their overwhelming numbers, those numbers created by new federal drug laws that made it highly profitable for even the lowest street peddler to make pockets full of money, which meant new prisons had to be built to hold them all, an impossibility, of course, because for every dope peddler they arrested there were two to take his place. So, if you're crying about not being able to find a job, try the Bureau of Prisons. Become a prison guard. Then you'll have it made from cradle to grave, for no profession on the face of the earth has a higher growth rate or better job security than they. And you don't have to have any qualifications other than the ability to stand on two feet and count to ten, in my admittedly biased estimation. For in my estimation there's room for dumb and dumber and *dumbest.*

There were some prison guards at Alcatraz, however, who didn't fit into any of those categories, like Lieutenant Mitchell (Fat Mitchell), and the old captain, whatever his name was, and even old Promising Paul, the sorry old warden who turned out to be not so sorry after all. They were real men, a dying breed, no, a dead breed, who carried themselves with respect and dignity and who deserve a place in the story of Alcatraz. And there were many prisoners who, despite being considered by society to be the worst of the worst, were nevertheless some of the best people I've ever known and some who I would learn to love like brothers before it was over.

And if these people, these "sorry" convicts, seem to be larger than life in my account of them, it's because they *were* larger than life. I mean, if you've ever wondered what happened to the outlaws when the Old West ceased to exist, well, they might have died and gone to Alcatraz, for the Alcatraz convict, for the most part, was different from the gang-banging prison "inmate" of today. We didn't fight each other, we fought the law. We stood on our own two feet. We usually lost, but at least we knew who to fight. And the prison guards had to take this into account when dealing with us. And they did.

But, like the Old West and the old convict, Alcatraz lived for a brief time and then died, and while a few accurate accounts of the history of Alcatraz have been written, the story of Alcatraz, how we lived, what we thought and said, who we were other than a name and number, is still largely a mystery.

So I guess it's up to me to fill in some of the missing pieces. This is a story of Alcatraz—and how I somehow managed to get there.

CHAPTER ONE

On a cold and foggy January morning in nineteen-fifty-seven I took that boat ride across the San Francisco Bay to Alcatraz, involuntarily because I was a prisoner, not a tourist. I was cuffed and shackled and wore a standard issue shirt and pants three sizes too big for my skinny frame, and I was scared shitless. Scared not particularly of Alcatraz, though there was that too, but scared because of my most immediate danger which was that the raggedy boat on which I so helplessly rode was sure to capsize any second and send me straight to hell long before my time to go there. I was only twenty-three years old, much too young to die.

I remember clearly how I hung on desperately to that boat seat between my legs and how the boat bobbed up and down in the swelling black water and how my steel cuffs bit into my wrists and ankles. I had never in my life been on a boat on any body of water larger than a small pond, and the fog made the distance to shore, any shore, seem endless, for I could not see land in any direction. Up and down the raggedy boat bobbed.

They had treated me shabbily from the beginning, waking me up from a sound sleep in the middle of the night in the hole of the U.S. Penitentiary in Leavenworth, Kansas where I had been a resident for the previous six or seven months. Then they had unceremoniously dressed me out in the shabby clothing I still wore and which still didn't fit properly. And while I was still half asleep they told me I was on my way to Alcatraz. Huh?

Who, me? Not me. There must be some mistake. I'm just a kid doing a four-year bit for car theft. All those thoughts went bouncing through my head from skull to skull without encountering a single cell of brain matter. It surely was a mistake. From Leavenworth they had driven me and three other prisoners in a prison van to a desolate spot out in the Kansas farmland where we were transferred to a bus driven by U.S. Marshals, and then we were transported still in darkness to Wichita and put on a train headed west. We had a special train car all to ourselves, the four of us plus two marshals. The car had special bunks and its own bathroom. So I guess they were serious. I was on my way to Alcatraz.

And now I was in a raggedy boat just seconds from sinking to the bottom of the Pacific Ocean. Maybe they were taking us to Australia to labor in the swamps. Maybe we were lost on the high seas. Maybe—maybe shit, I was about ready to take over that boat. Too young to die, I was.

I looked around, seriously considering my options. There were four of us. We might have a chance. But Tex was chatting with the old man, both of them seemingly unworried about our fate, and the big Indian was sitting there silently as he had been for most of the trip. He had a big chip on both shoulders. Didn't they realize this silly boat wasn't going to make it? I mean this boat had reportedly made hundreds of safe trips between Alcatraz and the mainland, but not with me on it. And not across the Pacific Ocean, hopelessly lost as we were.

Then the fog parted and I saw it, finally, Alcatraz Island just ahead, saw the eerie light of the lighthouse making ghostly figures as it swept through the morning fog, saw the big haunted house atop that hill, and I think it was maybe then that I wished the boat would go ahead and sink after all. I didn't believe in ghosts, but Alcatraz Island on a foggy morning sitting (yes, sitting, not setting), Alcatraz Island sitting there like a living breathing thing ready to gobble us up right out of the water, clothing, handcuffs, boat and all—I can report with historical accuracy that I did not like that at all. And as I first beheld that sight my asshole was chewing a hole in the seat of my pants.

But the boat did not sink and the Thing did not gobble us up and we landed safely at last and with relief we were driven up the winding road to the main building which up close still was not pretty but not a ghost either. We were there.

The four of us were silent as they escorted us into the building and into a receiving area. They made us strip, bend over, turn around, lift 'em, the whole routine, nothing to it. But then they took us one at a time into a little room, and we got the real deal. An MTA stood there in a brown uniform flexing a rubber glove on one hand, and I didn't appreciate that at all. It was what they did at Alcatraz, but not at any other prison that I know of, a special greeting for all arriving Alcatraz prisoners: Ye old fingerwave.

We weren't happy about that.

Next, wearing a bathrobe we were led into an office one at a time for an initial interview with a stern lieutenant who when I went in was studying some papers on his desk. I came to a stop in front of his desk and stood there waiting—they always make you wait awhile without acknowledging your presence just to show you who's boss, I guess. He finally looked up. "Baker?"

"Yes sir," I answered neutrally, not a smart-ass but not condescending either.

He studied me, a hint of surprise crossing his face. "How old are you?"

"Twenty-three," I answered sadly.

"What are you doing here, you're a little young aren't you? What are they doing, robbing the cradle these days?" He shuffled some papers and began reading something. Then he read out loud: "...cut your handcuffs off on the transfer bus from McNeil Island to Leavenworth...ran a boxcar through the rear gate of the Oregon State Prison...hit a guard with a stick during a prison riot..." His face really clouded up when he read that last bit of information. He continued reading silently, his face turning darker by the minute until he finally slammed the report down on the desk and looked at me again, just sat there looking at me.

I stood silently. Was he talking about me?

Finally, without another word, he wrote something on a card and sent me out of his office.

When they finished processing us I had a brand new prison number, 1259-AZ, me. Then dressed in bathrobes we were herded down into a large open shower room in the basement where we showered and picked up our issue of new prison clothing, sheets and blanket and stuff, tooth powder, razor, soap, and last a set of metal earphones which we were cautioned to hang onto and take care of or else we'd have to pay for them. Then upstairs we went with our bundles. In the cell house we stopped at a guard desk.

The guard at the desk must have been the cell house officer, the number one, because our escorts handed him a set of cards and said, "Four new ones for you."

The guard at the desk took the cards and studied them, then called out our names one at a time. When he called my name I answered and he looked up at me with surprise. "What are you doing here? How old are you?"

"Twenty-three," I answered sadly.

"They must be hard-up for recruits. What did you do, rob a bubble-gum machine?" And he laughed at his joke.

"I stole a car," I answered innocently. Tex rolled his eyes. The old man chuckled.

"You stole a car?" He shook his head. "What is the world coming to, they're sending us car thieves."

Finally he assigned us to our cells, took us down "Broadway," a wide corridor between two rows of cells. He locked us down still shaking his head.

All cells at Alcatraz were one-man cells with a bunk on one

wall and a small fold-down desk on the other. There was a toilet and sink and some shelves on the back wall and open bars in front. Standard prison design. I tried my sink, only one faucet handle, just cold water, no hot, not standard prison design. I found a plug-in for my earphones on the wall. It worked. I sat on my bunk. Home.

The horror stories we'd heard about Alcatraz were not exactly true, as I found out when they finally let me out of my cell and I hit the yard for the first time, or at least that's what Benny Rayburn told me. He ate at our table in the mess hall so I was already acquainted with him. People at the table were always asking him questions about the law, which he seemed to be able to answer easily, so I guess he was some kind of jailhouse lawyer. Anyway I was wandering around looking like I'd just rode in on a mule, so for whatever reason he struck up a conversation with me. He was friendly enough, congenial and all that, but what caught my ear was the way he talked on and on so clear and logical without using a single cuss word. I mean I could tell right away that he wasn't a hard-headed convict because most of us real convicts couldn't even talk without using fuck words.

He told me the most dangerous threat on the island was getting splattered with seagull "poop," as those birds were everywhere, dropping their loads in mid-flight without discrimination. As for the threat of physical danger from another prisoner, the stories were mostly false, he said. In the first place there were only about two-hundred and fifty prisoners at Alcatraz at any one time and when you were out of your cell you were hardly ever out of sight of a guard. You never went anywhere without being escorted by a guard.

And he said there were no gang-bangers at Alcatraz. All prisoners were individuals who stood on their own two feet. Gang-bangers in federal prisons were a thing of the distant future. There were barely enough convicts at Alcatraz to get up a good softball game. That doesn't mean there weren't some bad boys at Alcatraz, there were. But they didn't go around stabbing people just for the fun of it. And when there was trouble at Alcatraz it was between two men and they took care of business and that was the end of it one way or the other.

The only gang-bangers at Alcatraz were the guards themselves, he went on, especially the goon squad. They didn't take no "crap." They didn't go around messing with people either. You could holler at them, cuss them out, snivel like a baby, whatever, they'd just write you up and keep on going, but God help you if you laid a hand on one of them. They'd beat your brains out. A good example of that is what happened to the big Indian who rode the train to Alcatraz with us. They put him in the hole when they found a knife in his cell. He hollered and cussed and swore the knife wasn't his. He threw a big fit when they got him to the hole. No problem. But when he caught a guard too close to his cell and knocked him senseless with a single blow the goon squad rolled in on him. He was big and he could fight which he proved without a doubt when they rushed into his cell. He whipped about half of them, but they called in reinforcements and when they got him down they beat the sawdust out of him. When they were through they sent what was left of him to the Medical Center for Federal Prisoners in Springfield, Missouri where he was placed in the maximum security nut ward. There, they turned him into a vegetable by applying the appropriate combination of chemicals to appropriate places on his big body. Some say they eventually killed him. That's what they say. I don't know, but I do know we never saw him again. And if you don't believe this, look him up. His name is Bruce Allmond, listed on the Alcatraz roster as white but he was at least part Indian and he was sent to Alcatraz for assault on another inmate with intent to commit murder while at the federal institution at Terre Haute, Indiana.

All I know is that he disappeared from the face of the earth and his disappearance probably wasn't aided by ghosts. So you figure it out.

So the guards didn't take no "crap," Benny Rayburn went on to explain, if you laid a hand on one of them, but, on the other hand, there was nothing petty about most of the guards at Alcatraz; leave them alone and they'd leave you alone. Do your time and they'd do theirs.

There were exceptions to that, of course, guards who went out of their way to mess with everybody every chance they got for little petty things. It was one of those that I was bound to run into by my very nature, and run into him I did. But I'll tell you about him later.

Another reason there was little violence at Alcatraz was there was little to fight over. There was no commissary, nothing to buy even if you had all the money in the world. The food you got in the mess-hall was all you got. It was good food, the best of any prison food in the country, for the warden believed in feeding his prisoners. It was said that a past warden named Johnson had started that custom, of feeding good, because, as hard-nosed as he was, he was wise enough to know that most riots and strikes in prison populations were caused by bad food. The new warden, Paul Madigan, continued that practice. It made sense. But still, there was no commissary, so you'd better not miss any meals, which I didn't.

And there were no drugs to fight over for the simple reason that there were no drugs, period, unless you figured aspirin to be a drug. There were a few prisoners on thorazine or a terrible mixture called green lizard, but not because they wanted to be. So drugs were not a factor in causing trouble at Alcatraz.

And punks, homosexuals, well, there was a killing once in a while over that, every couple of years maybe. But there wasn't much to be done about that. Hell hath no fury like the wrath of a jilted punk (my contribution to the conversation with Rayburn).

Gambling? Of course most of us did some of that. The institution gave us three packs of Wings a week, passed out a pack on Monday, Wednesday and Friday. They must have had a million cartons of those cigarettes stored away in a huge warehouse somewhere, because that's what we got for all the time I was there. And you could get all the Bull Durham you wanted for free from a rack on the cell house wall to take up the slack. We gambled with the cigarettes, football games, baseball, basketball, a pack here a pack there, nothing heavy enough to fight over. So gambling wasn't a big problem.

Our most valuable possession was the Christmas bag they passed out every year on Christmas Eve, Benny explained with such relish that my mouth started watering before he got half through. Since we never got any candy or snacks of any kind, that Christmas bag was a great big deal. And it was worth fighting over. But more about that later, too.

Anyway, I remember well the first day they let me out of my cell for recreation. I hit that yard with much anticipation, so glad was I to get out of that cell, for the bad thing about Alcatraz was not physical, it was mental, the long boring grind of being locked down day and night for days at a time, of enduring the unrelenting boredom. That was it, just plain boredom. I can't think of another single word that better describes it. So I came out of that cell and hit the yard like a horse out of the stable. And I saw the sunshine and felt the fresh air on my face for the first time in many months, and I let out a silent whoop of joy.

While Benny Rayburn was talking I was half-listening and half surveying my new surroundings. The yard, my yard now, was small. There was a wall around it, not tall enough to keep a guy from standing on another guy's shoulders and grabbing the top and bounding right over it, but the wall had a fence on top of it running all the way around, and there was a guard shack in one corner and a guard walking around on a catwalk. And they had guns up there. No thanks.

At one end of the yard two shirtless convicts were playing a game of handball, smacking the small ball against the higher wall there. Beyond the handball court prisoners walked back and forth, ignoring a softball game that was underway and which sent an oversized softball soaring in the air and landing with a smack among them. I guess they were used to that for they paid it little attention. An outfielder scrambled between the walkers to retrieve the ball and threw it toward the infield. I asked a guy why they used such a large ball and was told the yard was so small that they had to use a larger ball that wouldn't fly over the wall every time somebody hit it good.

Next I wandered over to the other end of the yard, just sort of moseyed along looking at this and that and enjoying the sunshine and the smell of salt air coming from the sea. Behind the batter's box was a high metal screen and behind that were the card tables. I was surprised to learn that most of the prisoners were playing bridge, and that's something I'd never seen before in the places I'd been locked up in, bridge.

I watched for a while. They were using what looked like dominoes as cards, shuffling them face-down on the table like dominoes, but they were actually a little bigger than dominoes, I think, and were made of ivory or plastic or something, and each player was dealt thirteen of them which were then held in a wooden holder and sorted by suit—red was hearts, black was spades, green was clubs and yellow was diamonds, the colored spots I mean. Sort of like rook, I guess, and at first I thought that's what it was, but somebody told me no, they were playing bridge. Beat all I ever saw, a bunch of raggedy convicts playing bridge.

On long high concrete bleachers overlooking the yard were convicts with their easels and brushes, painting pictures of the Golden Gate Bridge, or the bay, or the San Francisco waterfront in the distance. I saw all this as I moseyed about peeping over their shoulders. High on the bleachers as they were they could see out over the little wall on the other side of the yard and see all that they were painting. They were painting freedom.

Nobody was painting anything that was going on down on the yard.

And up on the bleachers a couple of guys were banging on acoustic guitars, while others were just hanging out on the bleachers doing nothing. None of the guys on the bleachers, neither the artists nor the guitar players nor anybody else, paid much attention to the fly balls that careened their way or the seagulls dumping their loads. I guess they just accepted it as part of the routine. Everybody had a routine, I guess, even the seagulls.

Me, I didn't have a routine yet and I vowed not to get one for as long as I could avoid it, for I had learned to stir up a little shit once in a while to combat the monotony. Once you settled into a routine and surrendered to the comfort of the bells, a bell to eat, a bell to go to sleep, a bell to go to work, a bell for everything—once you surrendered to the comfort of the bells your soul belonged to the warden. I wasn't smart, maybe, but the zigzagging road to Alcatraz had taught me that much.

Actually, we woke up to the recorded wake-up call of a bugle, and went to bed to the sound of a bugle playing taps, but I refer to the bells symbolically because institutions normally use bells for everything. And anyway a bell is a bell.

*****

CHAPTER TWO

A water tower rises high above Alcatraz Island shivering on long iron legs in the cold January wind. They have to bring in water on a water boat, because they have no fresh water on the island. From the boat the water is somehow sucked up into the belly of the tower where it is cooled by the winter wind to an appropriate temperature to send shock waves through the body of any Alcatraz prisoner who dares splash it on any part of himself from the sink from which it flows.

Me, I remember well those first January mornings after my arrival when I crawled out of bed in the morning and prepared my face for shaving, how that first splash of water set my teeth to chattering and sent goose bumps down the entire length of my skinny body from head to toe. Keeping a clean shave was mandatory for us convicts. It was a rule strictly enforced. A short haircut was also enforced, but it was the icy water on my face that I remember most.

It was on such a morning after my arrival that a middle-aged man in a suit stopped in front of my cell. He identified himself as the librarian. He also introduced himself as the parole officer. As the librarian he explained the rules of the library and gave me a library card and a catalog of books in the library. I was instructed to fill out the card and give it to the inmate when he made his rounds with the library cart. As the parole officer he told me no one had ever made a parole from Alcatraz and never could expect to, therefore I might just as well sign a waiver saying I didn't want to make a personal appearance before the parole board, and he just so happened to have such a waiver with him with my name already typed in and a big X where I was to put my signature. I only hesitated a minute. With my prison record I couldn't expect to make a parole even if I grew a halo and a set of white wings. And I only had a few years left on my sentence anyway. So I signed it.

After he left I looked through the library catalog. They had every book ever written by Zane Grey. So I wrote them all down on my library card. I'd have something to read for a while.

On the yard I met Punchy Bailey. I'd known him up in the state pen in Oregon, well I'd known him a little bit, known of him. I'd never actually talked to him. He was the warden's clerk in Oregon and we hardheads didn't associate with inmate politicians, which is what we labeled him up there, a politician. As the beleaguered Warden O'Malley's clerk he had smoothly worked himself into a position of effectively running the whole penitentiary, he, Punchy Bailey. After the big riot which got O'Malley fired, the new warden, The Gimp, himself, sent Punchy Bailey straight to Alcatraz. He wasn't about to leave anybody around as smart as Punchy Bailey.

I didn't recognize Bailey at first, I hadn't known him all that well, but he recognized me and he cut into me walking the yard and made some laps with me explaining his former role as the warden's clerk in which he smoothly painted himself as a champion of his fellow inmates, changing their cells when they needed a change, changing their work assignments, getting their girlfriends placed on their visiting list, all free of charge, he said. He was a good talker, and seemed honest to me, though I think I knew better, but when he was finished I believed him. He was that good.

It didn't make any difference to me, anyway. He was liked and respected at Alcatraz so I left it that way.

And to demonstrate his good will toward me he told some people who told some people of my good reputation which he could vouch for first hand, for I had done more than two years in the hole up there in Oregon, two years in the hole as a stand-up convict, and two years on the yard raising hell and going back to the hole. So I brought a lot of respect with me to Alcatraz. And while I was no Al Capone or Machine Gun Kelly I could walk any prison yard, including Alcatraz, with my head held just as high as anybody.

Next, I met two men, two convicts who I would know for life, who I would run across again and again in other federal prisons after Alcatraz was closed and who I would learn to love like brothers.

The first was Forest Tucker, a congenial man about fifteen years older than me who was the leader of the Alcatraz band. I liked him from the beginning. I had played a little in the prison band up in Oregon, guitar. I explained to Tucker that I couldn't read music but I knew my chords and had a good ear, so I could probably figure out the songs and follow along. Well, Forest Tucker just laughed and said nobody in the band was a professional, that they just played for the fun of it. They practiced on Saturday mornings down in the basement shower area and I was welcome to come on down.

Tucker was a bank robber. That's what he was, what he did when he was on the streets. When he was in prison he played music and walked the yard and talked about robbing banks with anybody who would listen. When he was free he robbed banks. Can't fault a guy for that. He just liked to rob banks.

I made some laps with him walking and talking about music. I guess he was on his good behavior for he just talked about music when we first met, didn't mention robbing banks a single time. That must have been very hard for him. But Tucker had such an unassuming, infectious personality that I would have listened to him no matter what. He was easy to talk to and listened to me with such honest interest that we spent over an hour just walking and talking that first day I met him.

My favorite musician, of course, was Elvis Pressley, that twanging electric guitar in his band. Tucker said his favorite band was Benny Goodman. That clarinet. But he said he was learning to play piano so he'd have something to play when he no longer had the wind to play sax or clarinet. That amazed me that he could plan so far in the future. Me, I could barely see past tomorrow and if I ever lived to be fifty I hoped somebody would shoot me for being so old.

And when I mentioned that I wanted to learn how to play bridge he introduced me to the second man who was later to become my friend. That man was Dick Bayless, officially John Richard Bayless, but everybody called him Jackrabbit. They called him that because he tried to escape a couple of times, jumped right in the water the first time and was swimming straight for San Francisco when they plucked him up like a wet dog and brought him on back to Alcatraz. He told me he had expected them to shoot him, even hoped they would if he didn't make it, but I guess they had other plans for him, they and Federal Prison Industries, for he was a good worker and FPI always needed good workers.

He tried to escape again when he went back to court over in San Francisco for his first escape. He again was captured without getting shot. He could neither win nor lose.

When I met Jackrabbit he was a quiet, patient man. Tall and slender, he carried himself with the quiet dignity of a man who had died and come back to life two times and had finally said fuck it, and after that he settled down, got him a routine, worked in the factory business office, and became the best bridge player in Alcatraz.

To show you how patient he was, he played chess by mail with this guy over in Europe somewhere. They played for years, back and forth, each move taking two or three weeks, maybe a month. And he told me one day he figured by the time they played about ten more games his time would be up and he'd be free. That's how patient he was.

Anyway they still called him Jackrabbit, settled down or not, which, to me, wasn't a fitting name for a man brave enough to jump into those dangerous waters, suicidal intentions or not, for he had a quiet elegance about him that contradicted such a frivolous nickname. And, besides, I think I knew how he felt because I, myself, had rode that boat to Alcatraz on a foggy January morning.

But now he had him a routine. He played bridge on the yard at Alcatraz, content, the dying embers of life lingering on his face, life as we know it fading.

Forest Tucker and Jackrabbit, Dick Bayless, had a lot in common. For one thing, they both had respect. They had the inner toughness to endure the daily grind of prison life. They didn't have to demand respect from other convicts by outward displays of muscle and noise like monkeys in a jungle, as many prisoners did. Theirs was an inner strength of character, and respect came their way naturally in bits and pieces over a period of time. But make no mistake if you get the idea they were weak. I knew them back then. For there was a day at Alcatraz when they both stood up when it counted most. It was the real deal, and I never doubted them after that.

In Alcatraz we were friends, me and Jackrabbit and Tucker, though we didn't hang out a lot together. I tried to play bridge with Jackrabbit, as his partner. That didn't work out too well. He fired me. But he gave me a book on bridge by Eli Culbertson and told me to study it and he'd see me later.

So I studied the book and got me a partner and challenged Jackrabbit and his partner to a game. I'd show his smart ass.

They beat me unmercifully. That's when I first started to realize Jackrabbit wasn't as soft as I first thought he was, for he was deadly on the bridge table. Like I'd made a little bid of three-no-trump or something, knowing I had a lock because I had a whole hand full of aces and kings and such, and he'd quietly doubled me and I'd snickered inwardly as I took his opening lead, and then, suddenly and unbelievably, he'd torn my skinny ass up. I mean, he didn't grin or brag or anything, he just quietly tore my ass up. Down four, doubled and vulnerable.

Son-of-a-bitch.

When I say Jackrabbit was quiet I don't mean John Wayne

quiet, for he didn't swagger or carry a big stick, and I don't mean sneaky quiet like a few people I'd known. And he wasn't softly quiet, like Simpco, who was the nicest guy in the world but would kill you in a second on principle. Jackrabbit was just thoughtfully quiet. Like even when he was silent, which was most of the time, you knew something was going on up there in his head.

But then I saw another side of him one day in the mess hall when somebody was kidding him about his beloved Boston Red Socks. He could get excited about that—and loud at times in defense of the slumping Sox. And you'd better not bad-mouth Ted Williams. That was after Ted Williams came out of the military and batted four-hundred for the season, so he was still greater than God in Jackrabbit's mind.

Some people took advantage of Jackrabbit's loyalty to his team, knowing he'd take any bet offered, so they'd get him worked up and then bet him a pack of cigarettes on the day's game, or two packs or three.

It was hard for me to watch these snickering fools take advantage of Jackrabbit the way they did, but this was before I got to know him all that well, and anyway he was a grown man, so it wasn't any of my business. Boston was really losing bad that year, game after game, and Jackrabbit would lose his cigarettes and turn right around and bet on the bums again. He must have loved them a lot. Jackrabbit didn't smoke, that was one thing, but still, cigarettes were worth a lot in our little world.

You couldn't have but three packs of cigarettes in your cell, that was the rule, so we took our extra cigarettes down to the factory and hid them there just to play it safe. I mean most of the guards didn't bother about extra cigarettes or little petty stuff like that when they shook down our cells. They'd bust you if they found a knife or some homemade hooch, or something like that, but if it wasn't serious they didn't mess with it. But there was always that ass-hole who went by the book trying to make some brownie points.

I ran into one of those one day. It was a Saturday morning and the sun was shining bright outside. I was ready to hit the yard. That was really a big deal in Alcatraz, the yard. We got yard rec on Saturday and Sunday during the day. That was it. And that was only when it wasn't raining. And we only got Sunday morning rec every two weeks, because every other week they showed a movie on Sunday morning after church. So that Saturday morning I was bouncing off the wall ready to get out of that cell.

Well, when the doors slid open mine didn't slide. At first I didn't know what was going on because people were walking by my cell on the way out and my door was still closed. I tried to open it but it was locked tight, so I started hollering, thinking there was something wrong with my door. "Tell the guard my door didn't open!" I yelled at the passing prisoners. Which did no good at all. And when everybody was gone, a young, fresh-faced guard appeared in front of my barred door.

"I'm writing a disciplinary report on you for having too many cigarettes in your cell. You had four packs, which I confiscated and which I'll turn in with my report. You'll remain in your cell until you go to court." That's what he said standing there in front of my cell.

I went nuts on him. I mean, I wouldn't be able to go to court until next week sometime. The whole weekend would be over with me locked in my cell. I called him every dirty name I knew. Well he turned a little red but then he just took out a pen and pad and started writing down everything I said.

I finally ran out of breath and slumped down on my bunk, still steaming while he finished writing. Now I'd go to court for having too many cigarettes and cussing him out too. It's a good thing for both of us that the door was locked or I would probably be in even worse trouble. I checked my stash and sure enough my cigarettes were gone, all four packs of them. "Hey, you took all four packs. I only had one pack over the limit. You're only supposed to take that one!"

Well, he just gave me an indulging look and said, "Okay, I thought of that, but I couldn't determine by looking at them which one was the extra pack. They all looked the same. So I had to take all of them to make sure I got the right one."

Yes, he actually said that. I remember every word like it was yesterday. I was so surprised that I couldn't speak. I mean it was so ridiculous I just sat there looking at him. And he turned and left.

I wish I could think of his name, but I can't. I think it was Simmons, but I'm not sure. Somebody told me they thought he came to Alcatraz from El Reno or one of those youth joints. They've really got some petty rules in reformatories, and he acted like that's where he came from, so maybe he did. So I'll call him Simmons for the sake of this, because that wasn't the last time I, we, ran into him. He messed with me and everybody else for the whole time I was there.

Whitey Knight celled next door, so he handed me over a pack of cigarettes and a pack of Bull Durham so I'd have something to smoke. And Jackrabbit sent me up a bridge book with the chapters marked on defensive card play and defensive bidding, so I guess he was trying to tell me something about my game.

I would go to the hole for cussing old Simmons out. I was a goner for sure. I wasn't afraid of the hole, or anything like that, but to tell the truth I sort of dreaded it, the monotony mainly. And I wouldn't be able to smoke. And they might even keep me in segregation after I did my hole time. They probably would. I'd really cussed out old Simmons pretty good, and he'd wrote it all down. And when they write it down like that they always make it sound twice as bad as it really is. So I was gone for certain.

Court day came Tuesday and a full lieutenant came to escort me down to their little kangaroo courtroom. He stuck his head in to let them know I was there and then we waited outside. He was a different lieutenant than the one who interviewed me when I first came in and he didn't seem like such a bad guy. We talked for a while, and he asked me some questions about what I did, so I told him straight out about the cigarettes and stuff and about cussing Simmons out. When I was through he advised me to explain it like that when we went into the room. "Just be straight with them, the captain don't like bull shitters." I learned later that his name was Lieutenant Mitchell. They called him Fat Mitchell, and like I said, he wasn't such a bad guy.

When they called us in I saw a guy in a captain's uniform and a guy in a suit and tie who I figured was an associate warden or something, both sitting behind a desk. The guy in the suit started off talking and then turned it over to the captain who on that day did most of the talking. It was what he said that I remember most clearly because he talked in a language I could understand, not the bullshit language of many of the officials in suits.

"William Baker?"

"Yes." They didn't offer me a chair, so me and the lieutenant stood there while the captain studied some papers. He read out the charges, out loud, the extra cigarettes, all the cuss words and some extra ones I don't remember saying. Then he looked up at me curiously. "How old are you?"

"Twenty-three," I said sadly.

Well the old captain really surprised the hell out of me. His face sort of softened and he chuckled. "You can wipe that pitiful look off your face, Baker. I know who you are. I've got your institution record from Oregon and your FBI file and I've read every word of both of them. You were a bad boy up in Oregon, weren't you? Broke out of the hole—you and five other inmates took six prison guards hostage and made them push you down a hill in a boxcar, where you rammed it through the back gate with bullets flying—is that true?"

That was true. I just nodded and mumbled something.

"You had thirty-two disciplinary reports while you were there, one for hitting a guard with a stick during a prison riot, and here you are, still alive. You must have had a very understanding warden up there."

The tone of his voice wasn't threatening but his words were. I didn't know what to say so I said nothing.

He went on, "Did you have a very understanding warden up there?"

He was pushing it. I decided to be honest. "Yes, I guess so. Some guards wanted to shoot us but he wouldn't let them. But we didn't like him. We called him old Beet Face, because his face was always turning red when he got excited." I hesitated, went on. "I guess we didn't appreciate him till we got rid of him and an old gimp-legged warden from the feds took over. He wasn't no joke."

"Well, we've got a very understanding warden here, too. Have you met Promising Paul?"

"No, not yet." Where was he going with this?

"The prisoners call him that because he sometimes makes promises he can't keep, like helping you get off this island, which he can't do because that's determined by the Bureau of Prisons, but he does try. And if you hit one of my guards with a stick or any other weapon there's nothing he can do to keep you from getting a serious ass-whipping, either, because that's determined by my goon squad who will pay you a visit over in the hole and take turns whipping you until they get tired and then they'll rest and whip you some more. They'll hurt you Baker, and they won't clean up the mess. And when they're all through they'll send an MTA down to tend to your wounds, but you won't get any sympathy from him. He'll just give you a couple of aspirins and tell you to drink plenty of water and walk slow. Do you understand that?"

I could feel my face turning red, and I was about to say something, but he cut me off.

"But I've got a good idea. You've only got a couple of years left—why they sent you here I don't know—but you ought to be able to do that little bit of time standing on your head, so if you don't fuck with us we won't fuck with you."

That threw me off balance, and before I could think of

anything to say he went on, changing the subject. "I see you haven't got anyone on your visiting list. Do you ever hope to get a visit from anyone while you're here?"

"I don't know anybody except my mother and she's too far away," I said.

"In Kentucky?"

The fucker knew everything, and he wasn't reading from any papers. "Yes."

"Do you ever wonder why you don't know anyone who might be able to visit you?"

I felt my blood pressure rising again, but I held my mouth shut. Was he testing me, to see if I'd go off? Again, his voice wasn't menacing but his words were. I mean I had a temper, but I wasn't suicidal. I just didn't know how to take this, uh, captain. He sounded more like a convict.

He let me think about that for a minute, and when I didn't answer he finally turned to the papers on his desk. "Okay, Officer Simmons wrote a very colorful report on you—what do you have to say about that?"

I shrugged. "I'd been waiting all week to go to the yard. It was Saturday morning, the sun was shining, and I was ready to go. And then my door didn't open. That fucked me up."

When I didn't say anything else, he turned to the guy in the suit and asked him if he had any questions or comments. The guy cocked his head at me for a minute, but then he declined.

"Okay," the captain said. "Officer Simmons used improper procedure when he shook you down and took all your cigarettes, but on the other hand you dressed him down pretty good, so we could call it either way."

He opened his desk drawer and pulled out four packs of Wings bound in a rubber band, which he looked at and played with for a minute, then he took one pack of them and dropped it back in his drawer. The other three he slid across the desk in my direction. "This is your first report, so I guess we'll let you slide. Don't let me see you back in here again anytime soon."

He looked at Lieutenant Mitchell. "Take him back to the cellblock. Tell the CO to take him off lockdown."

Were they turning me loose? Holy fucking shit, they were turning me loose.

Lieutenant Mitchell looked at me and nodded at the door. I mumbled some kind of thanks and headed that direction.

The captain said, "Don't forget your cigarettes." So I whirled around and grabbed my smokes, trying not to grin.

The captain added, "Write your mother. You never know when you might need her someday."

His words bounced off my head and I didn't think about that until later. Right then I got the fuck out of there.

*****

CHAPTER THREE

A lollypop sunrise came up over Alcatraz as we fell in on the yard in work-detail groups and went down the steep winding steps to the factory shops single file.   Happy thoughts frolicked in my brain like warm puppies. This was my first day on the job.

Lollipop sunrise? Yep. The day before they'd assigned me to a job in the glove shop and that meant I would no longer be locked in my cell all day during the week. You had to have a job to get out of your cell except when the yard was open on the weekend. And to go with the job they'd moved me to a new cell over on the bright side of C-block with the rest of the factory workers, and lucky me my new cell was on the second range near the front and I could see out the window, see the sea, see the sky, feel the fresh air when the windows were open. So, yes, it was a lollipop sunrise.

Happiness comes in small packages in prison. But it comes. It has to get through the gray filter of awareness that you're locked up. But it gets through, somehow, maybe not as powerful as cruising down the road with the wind at your back and all your red lights green, like when you're free, but it gets through in smaller portions. It's all relative. To a junkyard dog a bone is pure heaven.

And, me, I was locked up, all right, but there was nothing wrong with my chemistry, with my hormones, whatever

Mama Nature endows us with to keep our nuts pumped up. I was just naturally happy, always had been. I mean there were no warm puppies to hug at Alcatraz, no one to hold your hand. We were on our own. We got what we brought with us, and that's all we got.

There were no birthday parties for me, no touchdown dances. But it didn't take much to make me happy. Chemistry, I guess. All my sunrises came up lollipops. And if they didn't I knew how to stir up a little excitement.

Stop it, Baker!

Okay. I'm done.

Anyway, I bounced down those steps to the glove shop that lollipop sunrise morning for my first day of work. The boss introduced me to a sewing machine. Then he went into his office and sat. A convict introduced me to a box of white cotton gloves and showed me how to sew the front and back halves together to make a glove. None of it made any sense.

Two months later sitting at that same sewing machine it still didn't make a lot of sense, for I didn't see any point in sewing white cotton gloves, so I didn't break any records. I mostly just sat there daydreaming, thinking about this and that. One thing I could do good was daydream. My boss later wrote in one of his reports that I was the laziest man he'd ever seen, which didn't hurt my feelings at all. I had important things to think about, like the great mysteries of space and time and women—and what was for dinner.

Once in a while, though, I got a spurt of energy and sewed as fast as I could just for the hell of it. One day I sewed a whole box of gloves in less than an hour, really burned rubber. But I slowed down to my normal pace of one glove every once in a while as we neared lunch time.

The boss didn't care how fast we went anyway. We were on piecework and only got paid for what we did. And we couldn't buy anything with the money we made anyway. The boss, he just sat in his office and got up every half-hour or so to count heads, then he sat some more. He was pretty good at sitting.

Somebody said they counted every thirty minutes so we wouldn't have time to swim to the mainland between counts in case we were able to get out of the building and hit the water. Me, I didn't have enough time left on my sentence to risk another escape attempt. And, besides, those currents were really mean around the island, with two big rivers emptying into the bay close by. Sometimes you could see great big logs and things shoot straight up into the air and then disappear again and never come up. And they said the sharks around the island worked for the Federal Bureau of Prisons, wore badges and everything, which I, of course, figured was an exaggeration but I wasn't about to jump into that water to find out.

But it was neither the currents nor the sharks that posed the real danger. It was the temperature of the water in the bay. It was said that the average temperature of the water around Alcatraz Island was around fifty-five degrees and if you couldn't swim to the mainland in less than an hour your ass was history. Hypothermia. That was the main problem with escaping from Alcatraz. You'd freeze your ass off.

Yes, I know, people are swimming it routinely nowadays. A one-armed man swam it. A blind man swam it. A high-school class did it. Even a Golden Retriever dog swam it. But they trained in the Bay. They got used the cold water. And they wore wet-suits to insulate themselves against the cold. And they had a motor-boat cruising along beside them. We didn't. And we weren't trained.

However, one Alcatraz convict did swim it. He swam from Alcatraz Island all the way to Fort Point, the last stop along the coast before you came to the Pacific Ocean itself, the very last chance to grab onto a rock. He swam it. J. Paul Scott was his name. But that's another story.

It was spaghetti day at Alcatraz. My mouth watered thinking about it. The old Italian cook always started simmering his spaghetti sauce the day before and by the time it was done it was so good it would make you dizzy just thinking about it. Like I said, the old warden believed in feeding us. And the convict cooks took pride in their work. With the spaghetti they served an antipasta salad of some kind and a little dish of olives and anchovies, and we got a big dipper of butter beans and a big chunk of apple pie or something for desert. I mean they fed good. So we couldn't complain about the food.

Of course you could say they had to feed good because we couldn't buy any snacks or anything like you could in other prisons, so all we got to eat was what they fed us in the mess hall. You could say that. But we had plenty of things to complain about besides the food, so we left that alone.

Lunchtime finally came. I heard Lieutenant Mitchell coming down the factory street calling "Slow walkers!"

They took the slow walkers up the hill first, the old men and guys with a bad heart or lame leg. Then away we went, galloping up those winding steps to that spaghetti dinner."

Yes, I heard they turned the tables over later on in protest of the spaghetti, but that's because the old Italian guy left and they got another cook who didn't live up to our expectations when it came to cooking spaghetti. We were used to the good stuff.

*****

It was a slow, lazy summer that year. I played a little softball on a team of hapless scrubs. We barely knew what end of a bat to hold onto. We were so bad that we didn't even have a name. Finally somebody suggested we name ourselves after the cursed seagulls so despised by most people on Alcatraz Island, except me—I kinda liked them. So we called ourselves The Gullies, and we were really bad. We dropped balls that should have been caught, we struck out on big old fat balls right over the plate, we tripped over our own feet. But we had fun and a lot of people watched us just for the entertainment, sort of like watching the Keystone Cops, I guess. Me, I could run like a deer, I just couldn't hit the damn ball.

Forest Tucker was on our team. So was Whitey Knight, my next-door neighbor. They called him Whitey because he had premature gray hair and he was only about thirty-years old. And we had Fat Duncan and Jack Waites, great guys but they were both a little slow because they were still recovering from cutting their heel strings in protest over conditions over in the hole where they spent a good part of their time. So we took great pride in having a very fucked up team.

And that summer I finally got around to writing a letter to my mother. I wrote it mostly out of respect, because she was my mother, but we were never very close. My mother had given me up to my grandma when I was three-years old, and it was my grandma who had raised me. I loved her and she loved me, my grandma, and I cried when she died.

After that my grandpa got rid of me as quick as he could, found my mother and told her to come and get me. By then she had married Zeb Hackney, who was also from Kentucky, same county and everything, but she'd met him in Detroit working in a factory. A lot of people went to Detroit to find jobs in those days. Anyway, she came after me. I hid in a closet at my grandpa's house but they found me and took me away.

My mother explained to me that she'd had to give me to my grandmother because it was during the depression and Garnet, my father, had left her, and she, with no money and my baby brother in her arms—well, she'd had no other choice. She'd taken off to Detroit.

But that's another story, and I'm not here to trash my mother's name. She was still my mother.

In reform school I'd learned to respect my mother, for in reform school a mother's name was more sacred than a stack of bibles. If you took an oath on your mother's honor to prove to somebody you were telling the truth, then your word was accepted without question, and not even fingers crossed behind your back could negate such a sacred oath. And you'd dare not bad-mouth somebody's mother unless you were prepared to get into a serious fight.

So I wrote to her, my mother, something like, "Dear Mom, How are you, I am fine. I'm in Alcatraz. Your son, Bill." What else are you supposed to say to a mother? I had learned to respect her, but I had not yet learned to love her. Maybe that was something you couldn't learn.

And that summer Simmons worked the yard, the little guard I'd cussed out over the cigarettes. He was really pissed off when he first saw me on the yard. I guess he figured I'd be in the hole. When he first saw me his face turned red and he just kept looking at me, but I ignored him and walked away. He was a little guy, looked a lot like a girl. I figured maybe Mama Nature was having a problem with her X's and Y's, genetically speaking, when Simmons was conceived, and he could have been born a boy or a girl. It must have been a close call. Snicker.

Back in the cell that evening Whitey Knight handed me a magazine to read, figuring he was doing me a favor, but the magazine was *Reader's Digest* and I was not very fond of that magazine because of its views against convicts—they thought we should be treated even worse than we already were. Apparently they had never set foot on Alcatraz Island. But I thumbed through the magazine anyway until I came to a page that had been cut out by the old librarian, which pissed me off so I tossed it aside. The librarian was not only the librarian and the parole officer at Alcatraz, he was also the censor.

Prisoners were allowed to order a few magazines, like *Life* and *Look* and *Reader's Digest*. It was his job, the librarian, to read magazines that came in and cut out any article that dealt with crime or prison riots or any other excitable material that he deemed worthy of a good whack of his scissors. And whack he did, so that by the time you received your long-awaited magazine it often only served to make you so mad you couldn't read it anyway, so it went flying out the bars and over the tier.

Can you imagine censoring *Reader's Digest?*

Newspapers were forbidden entirely. So it was hard to get official confirmation of baseball scores and things like that, but, God bless him, our boss in the glove shop brought in a clipped-out copy of all the scores from the San Francisco newspaper every morning, which saved a lot of arguing about "I heard this" or "I heard that" on the radio. I wish I could remember his name, my boss. He was a decent man.

As the summer wore on the new started to wear off and the gray background in my head started turning a darker shade of gray. There was always that gray background. I mean you were always aware of where you were, no matter what you were doing. You could be watching a movie, listening to a football game, walking the yard, laughing and joking with your buddies, it didn't matter. Every thought in your head was filtered through that gray background of doing time. And when life in prison started to get boring it was my way to take action.

I decided, logically, that what our almost-barren recreation yard needed was a shade tree. And, logically, I decided it was up to me to plant one. So I did.

It wasn't a great big tree, or even a medium sized one. In fact it was a little sickly looking thing that I snatched, roots and all, from the side of the hill and shoved down the front of my pants and under my shirt as we came up the steps from work on a Friday afternoon. I hid it under my bed that night and the next morning I took it to the yard. I'd already decided where I was going to plant it. There was a spot over behind the screen behind the softball team benches that had a few sprigs of green stuff growing up next to the base of the screen, grass and weeds and stuff, so I dug a little hole, sneakily of course, and planted it there. I don't know what kind of tree it was, wasn't even sure it was a tree—it might have only been a bush—but, well, we'd find out in a year or so.

I had a little plastic bag like the ones Burgett made his water wings out of (and died in the bay when they collapsed), which I filled up with water from the drinking faucet, and I watered that tree and the grass and weeds around it.

Well, weeds need water too don't they?

I watered that tree every weekend, but it wasn't long before Simmons picked up on what I was doing and questioned me about it. "What are you doing, Baker?" he asked one day.

"Just watering the grass and stuff, uh huh." And I sprinkled the water all around, hoping he wouldn't notice my pitiful looking tree. Well, he just watched me doing what I was doing, and then he said, "Baker, you don't need to water that stuff, and look at all the weeds—you sure don't need to water them."

"Well, I know. It's just something to do." I shrugged and added, "And it can't hurt anything."

He studied for a minute and then walked off shaking his head.

I thought I'd fooled him, but I guess I hadn't, because that afternoon when we went back to the yard my tree was gone, roots and all. I knew it had to be Simmons, and he just wandered around, la-de-da, all afternoon and didn't look at me one single time, which was further proof, because any other time he'd be checking me out every ten minutes. There wasn't anything I could do about it, though, except bide my time and think of something else to do. Poor tree. It was uprooted long before it even reached puberty. What a shame.

I remember the first time I saw Robert Stroud, Birdman. Why they called him the Birdman of Alcatraz, I'll never know, because he never once had a bird while he was at Alcatraz. He had all his birds at the U.S Penitentiary in Leavenworth, but, oh well, the first time I saw him old Fat Mitchell was taking me from the factory to a dental appointment in the hospital one gray, misty morning , and we had to go through the yard to get there. And it just so happened that they were giving Birdman his one-hour-a-day of exercise, so I saw him standing on the other end of the yard, a gray ghost with a silver sheen around him as the sun, at that moment, came out from behind the clouds and tried to shine through the mist. He, Birdman, appeared like an apparition from another world, slouched forward with his hands in his pockets peering at me. Freaked me out, and for once in my life I was relieved to face a dentist rather than linger on the yard with that ghost.

And I remember well that first summer when one Saturday morning we couldn't go to the yard because it was pouring-down rain, Mother Nature doing her laundry, I guess. The bitch. I mean she could have picked a better day.

So we had a movie instead. Which would have been all right, except the preacher picked our rainy-day movies and we'd often see the same movie two or three times before he'd think to swap it for a new one. So between God and Mother Nature we just couldn't win.

I don't like church or funerals or hospitals. I used to go to church with my grandma, but when she died I had to go to all three and they didn't turn out too well at all for her. She died in a hospital and I saw her in a coffin in church and I saw them bury her in the graveyard. But I like graveyard cleanings and baptisms. At graveyard cleanings back home everybody brings big baskets of food, which they spread out on a bunch of tables placed end to end and we really chow down. I mean I used to go back and forth from one end to the other until my skinny stomach popped. But I didn't get in on any of the cleaning. That was before my grandma died.

And when the preacher baptized his flock we all went down to the creek to this special waterhole and sang songs for a while and then he'd do a little preaching but his sermon was short and then the good part came when he dunked the women all the way under and they came up dripping wet with their dresses clinging to their bosoms and — well, I was only seven but my eyes popped out just the same.

That was before my grandma died.

So I didn't go to church at Alcatraz, not that I didn't believe in God, I did, I just didn't go to church. And anyway somebody said the preacher went to gun practice with the rest of the guards so we figured he was a cop just like they were and he'd shoot us in a minute if he got a chance, though he might try to save our soul once we were dead.

I take it back, I did go to church one time while I was at Alcatraz. They held a memorial for Burgett when he died out in the bay, and I went then because he had that coming. He died but in dying he escaped from Alcatraz. He did that. He hit that water and they didn't bring him back alive. They brought back his body but his soul was long gone.

*****

CHAPTER FOUR

Burgett was a big boy, a strong boy, tall, slim of waist and wide of shoulders. He did pushups by the dozens and jogged the yard now and then when he wasn't playing poker. Told me he was in training, but he didn't tell me what for until a lot later. He was about five years older than me, I think, had a strong jaw and handsome face. He would have qualified for a part in a cowboy movie except for one thing: he was a knothead just like the rest of us, not dumb but not smart either. In fact, he would have been most qualified as a replacement for a team of mules on a Georgia chain gang.

So when someone suggested he join our raggedy softball team we jumped on it, for he was a perfect fit, a natural born Gullie. There was only one problem. He could smack that big old softball all the way over the wall every time. And a home run was counted as an out at Alcatraz. Don't ask me why. That's just the way it was.

He also worked in the glove shop and I got to be friends with him, so it was natural that when I decided to carry fruit from the mess hall to the glove shop to set up a batch of hooch, he quickly volunteered to help. I mean, it was time to stir up a little excitement, and I figured, logically, it was up to me to do it.

Some other guys volunteered to help, also. Carl Bistram, he got right in on it, wormed his way right in. Carl Bistram was usually dedicated to his work. He could really sew gloves, make that sewing machine sing songs all day long, and when he got through at the end of the day he was so covered with white glove dust from head to toe that he looked like Santa Claus, and everybody got out of his way when he went to blow himself off with the air hose. Well, he volunteered, too, with a thirsty look in his eyes, so I guess he had a secret taste for the bottle.

We tried to keep it quiet, but by the time we were through, half the glove shop was in on it.

I had learned a lot of good things up in Oregon, like how to make good home brew. A bowl of fruit, a pound of sugar, and a little yeast to each gallon of water was about right. The main thing, though, was the length of time you let it ferment before you tried to drink it. Seven days was about right, between seven and ten days. Leave it too long and it started turning to vinegar, drink it too soon and you'd get sick to your stomach. But, to tell the truth, what with all the shake-downs and the smell of fermentation, there was a bad risk of getting it busted, so you could, I mean you *could*, drink it in five days. Yep, you could.

So over a period of a couple of days each one of us carried whatever fruit we had with our meals, apples, oranges, plums, we carried them in the top of our socks down to the glove shop, and I got a packet of fresh yeast from the bakery for five packs of cigarettes, and by Friday we were ready to set it up, which I did, personally, in a trash can in the bathroom of the glove shop, I being the professional brew maker of the bunch.

We vowed we wouldn't touch it for five days, me and Burgett. That was it, five days.

Monday came and we went back to work. Somehow we'd made it through the weekend without cracking up from the suspense of waiting. We weren't there to watch it so anything could have happened to it, anything. After we filed into the shop and the boss settled down in his office, I cut my eyes toward the bathroom. I couldn't stand it any longer. I got up and made my way, nonchalantly, to the bathroom. Our garbage can was still there. I peeped inside, glanced back outside. A thousand eyes were on me, well, maybe ten or twenty, but it seemed like a thousand for they had stopped sewing and were flat out staring at me in the silence, frozen in mid-motion. I made a desperate pantomime of sewing motions until the idea finally got through to the dumb fuckers and they started sewing again. And again I peeped inside the garbage can, pulled out the big sack of trash that covered the bags of brew. It was still there! Yep, our brew was still there, bubbling like Niagara Falls, and the smell about knocked me over. I quickly re-covered it and made my way nonchalantly back to my seat. "It's still there," I whispered. Everybody stopped sewing to hear what I said. "Damn! Keep sewing. It's still there. It's okay!" I whispered as loud as I could. Everybody started sewing again, more vigorously this time.

That's exactly what happened. I remember it well. Looking back to that day in the glove shop on Alcatraz Island I wondered why the boss hadn't called a halt to the whole operation and locked us all up on the spot, for if he'd looked out his window and seen how hard all of us were working he'd have known without a doubt that something was wrong, something was bad wrong, because never in the history of Alcatraz had twenty sewing machines made such a racket, mine included.

But nothing happened, and we went to lunch and came back from lunch and still nothing happened.

Burgett eased over to my machine that afternoon and pretended to talk to me about a box of gloves I'd messed up. I told him to stack them on top of the other boxes of rejects I'd already got back from quality control, which amounted to about all the gloves I'd tried to sew that day. I guess Burgett had been thinking about our home brew that was bubbling away in the bathroom, that's what was really on his mind. And he finally got around to that. "I've been thinking. It's been five days since we set up our brew, and—we might ought to sample it and see if it ain't about ready to drink. I added it up and it's been five days. That was our agreement, five days, home-boy."

"How do you figure that?" I asked hopefully.

"Okay," Burgett counted on his fingers as he explained. "We set it up Friday, that's one day, and Saturday is two days, and Sunday is three days and this is Monday, so that's four days, and we started it early Friday morning and this is Monday afternoon, so that's five days."

He had used all four fingers and a thumb, so it came out to five days all right. I counted on my fingers, mouthing the words like he had, as he watched me anxiously, and, sure enough, I used all my fingers and my thumb. Then I counted my fingers and thumb, did the math and everything, and, yep, it came out to five days, and that was our agreement. "Yep," I said. "Five days." Whereupon I hopped up out of my chair and went straight into the bathroom and strained every bag of that hooch through two big bath towels and into one big bag. I threw the towels, mashed-up fruit and all, into the garbage can and covered it up quickly. Then I dragged the bag of hooch behind the garbage can and motioned triumphantly at Burgett to bring his cup, and he did, nonchalantly.

I sampled the first cup. It tasted good, a little sugary maybe, but good. Burgett sampled it, ran his tongue around his lips, smiled, and killed the whole cup. I slurped down a cupful. Wow. Told Burgett to send in Bistram. He did. Bistram drank a cupful, made a face. Everybody who was in on it took a turn, got up from their chairs one at a time and wandered into the bathroom nonchalantly, cool as hell. I drank another cup and wandered back to my chair, cool as hell and getting cooler by the minute, smarter too. I don't remember how many trips into that bathroom I took, but by late afternoon I was smarter than Einstein and the coolest convict on the planet. I'll never know how we got away with it.

Fortunately, we ran out of booze and somebody had sense enough to clean up the mess. Several times we had to scoot back to our chairs when the boss came out of his office to count heads, but he didn't even go into the bathroom, just glanced inside and kept on going. We were very lucky that day. Well, up to that point we were, because my luck ran out on the way up the steps. I forgot to tell you—I don't drink, not much anyway, because two beers makes me dizzy and three gets me drunk as hell, so Burgett had to help me up those steep stairs on Alcatraz Island that day.

My memory gets a little fuzzy here. I remember that we made it to the first landing, partway up the stairs. But Burgett had to turn me loose there because a big old guard was standing on the landing looking everybody over. Me, I must have tripped over something I guess because the next thing I knew I was on the ground and this big old guard was standing over me asking me questions and then he was hollering something and I looked at a pair of big old clod-hopper boots about level with my head which was about level with the ground, my head, and when I saw those big old boots I saw Zeb Hackney, my step dad, standing over me hollering crazy things and I stood up with an anger that not even alcohol could kill and I said, "Fuck you!"

That's when I discovered that my previous observation that you could cuss out the Alcatraz guards all day long and they'd just stand there writing down what you said, didn't always hold water. The guard standing there was a big old boy and when I said "Fuck you," that's all I remember because he threw a big roundhouse fist and I felt something hit my jaw and saw a blinding light, and he knocked me all the way into the next day.

I mean, I woke up in the hole and it was the next day so he must have knocked me there.

I was messed up. I remember that much. My jaw was sore, my head was sore, and when I tried to move I realized my ribs were sore, too, but I had to move and move I did, because the remains of that bubbling home brew had my stomach in a death-grip and I spent the rest of that day on or around my toilet bowl. It wasn't dark in my cell, that was a good thing, and I still had my clothes on so they hadn't thrown me in the strip cell.

The hole in Alcatraz only had one strip cell. That cell was dark, had a hole in the floor for a toilet and bread and water for food, except every third day you got a meal. The rest of the hole cells had a regular toilet and were provided with a mattress and blanket at night. Then the second and third tier of D-block, Segregation, had regular cells and were used for long-term isolation.

The MTA finally came down making his rounds. They let him in my cell. He looked me over good and cleaned my wounds, more sympathetic than I expected. He said my ribs weren't broken, though they sure felt like it. When he was through he asked, "How old are you?"

"Twenty-three," I answered sadly.

He shook his head sympathetically, but when he left all he gave me was some aspirin. He told me to take two aspirin, drink plenty of water and take it easy.

Take it easy? Like what else was I going to do? I was in the hole. But, oh well, take two aspirin, drink plenty of water and walk slow, the standard treatment for all prison ailments. They hadn't roughed me up too bad, just a few cuts and bruises here and there. They hadn't really given me the genuine ass-whipping that they were capable of, so the old MTA's magical remedy worked up to a point. I didn't die.

I waited and waited for them to come and get me and take me to court, hating to think what the old captain was going to say about it. Days went by.

As usual when I had to do hole time I retreated into my head, thinking about this and that. At first I let my brain go where it wanted to go, and as usual it landed on my secret question about time and space which I usually wondered about when I was doing hole time and which I never discussed with anybody else, especially not another knothead like myself, less they suggest I sign up to see the nut doctor.

I remember the first time I ever thought about it. I was about twelve-years old wandering around in the woods on Zeb

Hackney's hundred-and-twenty acre farm. I had got a good peek at Kathleen Vinson's pink panties that day in school when we were playing prison-base and she fell down and her dress went flying up in the air—but that's another story. Anyway, that day my brain was wondering about things it had never wondered about before, and as I lay on my back under a big tree and looked through the leaves at a patch of bright blue sky I wondered about space: if I went straight up and just kept going up, when would I come to the end of space, and when I came to the end would there be a wall there, and if so, what would be on the other side of that wall? So the great mystery began, of space and time, give due credit to Kathleen Vinson's pink underwear. And another great mystery began there too, for she was by far the prettiest girl in all of Caldwell County, Kentucky, maybe the whole world— and I thought about that too, those long glorious legs as she lay there with her dress all the way up above her hips.

Stop it!

Okay, I was in the hole in Alcatraz wondering about space and time, for by then I had figured, in my slow but dogged way, that space and time were somehow tied together, that they were even somehow related? The resemblance was remarkable: Space was forever, but that was impossible; time was also forever, but that was also impossible—the two great paradoxes of the universe. Einstein said if the answer to a question doesn't make sense you are probably asking the wrong question?

I sprained my brain trying to find that missing question, a hopeless task, about as hopeless as trying to figure out how I had wound up in Alcatraz.

The hole at Alcatraz was very boring. But it was about the same as the hole in other prisons. For one thing when you go to the hole your testosterone levels must drop all the way out of sight. Your libido dies completely. So thinking about sex is out of the question. Only a few basic instincts remain, maybe only one: Survival. I don't know. All I know is I retreat into my head. I think about space and time and how I got here. Not how I got in the hole or in Alcatraz or how I got into prison, but how I got *here*. Know what I mean?

But never mind that.

Guards came to let me out for a shower and I was given a razor and mirror to shave. I had been in the hole for about five days, I think, and I was hoping that letting me clean up was a sign they were getting me ready for kangaroo court. My bruises had turned a faded yellow, which meant they were healing fast. A convict in another cell told me I had been kicking and screaming when they dragged me into D block, and fighting like crazy, so I guess I was lucky to get off with just a light ass-whipping. I looked myself over real good in the mirror as I shaved. My face was okay, scratched up a little, bruised a little, but not bad.

One day a couple of guards came down and got me. I thought I was going to court, at last, but they escorted me into the cell house and put me in my old cell. I thought at first they'd made a mistake, so of course I didn't say anything. Then lunch came and they opened the doors and my door opened too. Holy shit! I jumped up and went to lunch with everybody else, and it was just like homecoming, everybody hollering at me and ribbing me and shaking my hand like I was really somebody. Burgett gave me a Gullie hug and him and the rest of my buddies loaded me down with smokes. The one good thing about going to the hole was getting out of the hole. It was like getting out of prison. And once I discovered I was really free I was happy as a dog with two, uh, tails.

That afternoon I went down to work with my crew, still wondering about not going to court or anything. They'd just turned me loose without a word. Benny Rayburn, our jailhouse lawyer, finally set me straight. He told me that the guard had hit me first, and that was illegal, even at Alcatraz. And he figured that since they'd given me a good ass-whipping they'd just left me in the hole until my bruises were visibly healed and then turned me loose, calling it even. And, sure enough, the next time I went to court for something else, they didn't even mention it, the getting drunk, the ass-whipping, nothing. It was like it had never happened.

I didn't complain.

And one day down in the glove shop I went into the bathroom and saw Burgett dunking a plastic bag full of air into a sink full of water. He was mashing on the bag to see if it would hold the air. He saw me but didn't say anything, so I didn't say anything.

But it didn't take a genius to figure out the only use for a bag full of air on Alcatraz Island.

CHAPTER FIVE

A seagull squalled a mating call. Or was that something inside me. I had seen a Doris Day movie that morning, and now I was up on the concrete bleachers looking out over the water at the San Francisco waterfront. It was an unusually clear day for the bay area and I could plainly see the tiny people, make out the women in bright colors. And seeing what I saw I had the most awesome revelation I'd ever had in my life, maybe even more awesome than the mind-blowing day Kathleen Vinson's dress flew up and I witnessed her glorious long legs all the way from her ankles to the Holey Land, maybe even more awesome than that. For I thought of all the women over there walking up and down, doing this and that, every one of them walking around with a pussy between her legs like it wasn't nothing, like it didn't mean a thing. I mean, there must be millions and billions of women in this world just walking around with a pussy between their legs like it didn't mean a thing. And here we were on Alcatraz Island, a bunch of raggedy-assed convicts who hadn't seen a woman in a long, long time. It fucked my head up.

I just had to tell somebody about my revelation, so I cornered Burgett and told him, explaining it just like it had come to me. He listened, all right, but when I was through he gave me a dumb look and said, "You've been locked up too long, Bill Baker," and he took off without another word.

So, okay, he was retarded, so I saw Jackrabbit and caught up with him walking. Maybe he would understand it, whereupon I explained it to him also as it had come to me.

Well, he listened and when I was through he didn't say anything but I know he was thinking about it because I could see the play of emotions on his face. Then he stopped walking for just a minute and glanced at the wall like he'd suddenly been awakened from a dream or something and I saw a sadness on his face, just briefly, and then it faded and he started walking again. I don't know what he was thinking and he didn't explain, but I knew he understood.

Which is more than I could say for myself, the understanding of it, because it had been revealed to me in the most basic form of knothead language to best fit my brain, but I knew it meant more than I could explain, the revelation.

Words like female companionship and love and loneliness come to mind, but that's something you don't talk about on Alcatraz Island. So pussy will have to do. I mean this is the story of Alcatraz. How we talked. How we lived. This is it. So if it's a little too much for you, I'm sorry; in that case the flowery language of the Reader's Digest version of prison life may be more suitable for you. For example, they are outraged that we get free dental care while they have to pay dearly for it. And they are distressed that we are not being more properly punished. "Are our prisoners being coddled?" they ask repeatedly and of course conclude that indeed we are, for reporters and politicians are constantly touring our prisons and noting that we are laughing and playing and seeming to be having a good old time, that we have movies and games and medical care and a factory where we learn good work habits (and get paid for it, for goodness sakes!). "I thought they were sent to prison to be punished for the crimes they committed, for goodness sakes! Are we coddling our prisoners?" And, of course we are, they conclude again, in a language embroidered with flowers to make it seem more convincing.

Well, okay, but let me tell you something, and I must tell you in terms reduced to the crudest language, for we had no flowers at Alcatraz, only weeds, so stop up your ears, if you must, because here it is, plain and simple: We were men. And we weren't getting any pussy. And that's the punishment. Get it, Reader's Digest? That's the punishment, maybe the most severe punishment ever inflicted by one human being on another, except for the loss of freedom itself.

Love is a four-letter word in prison, one you don't use when fuck will do, for you dare not show your weakness in the middle of a jungle where a spear may pierce that most vulnerable place in your heart. And loneliness is a word you never use even in a whisper.

Me, I loved my grandma and I loved my dog, and that's it. And I was never lonely except maybe sometimes in the privacy of my cell at night when I heard a tugboat chugging through a heavy fog and heard those foghorns bawing out in the bay. I mean I've heard a freight train whistle in the distance and I've heard a whippoorwill call, but nothing is lonelier than a foghorn calling out in the middle of the night from a cell on Alcatraz Island. Nothing except maybe Elvis Presley singing Heartbreak Hotel on the radio. I'll never admit any of this in broad daylight, though.

Hold it, Reader's Digest! I'm not through with you yet. What about freedom, what about that? What about the loss of freedom, you who have no idea what freedom is, you who chain your family dog to a tree in your back yard and take it for granted that he's still going to wag his tail at the sight of you and lick the hand that throws him a bone. Do you think for one minute that he doesn't yearn with every breath to be off that chain, to be free? Yet he still jumps and plays in the small space that you've confined him to, so he must be happy.

Come back here, tourists and politicians and journalists, whatever you are; this is for you too! You who toured the plantations of the slave owners in the Old South and reported, "The darkies must be happy. See how they laugh and play? Why, they're like children."—you who have no idea what freedom is.

That's the punishment, get it?

The law reads: "I sentence you to prison as punishment for your crimes," *as* punishment, not *for* punishment. It means: "As punishment for your crimes, I sentence you to lose the most precious thing in your life, I sentence you to lose your freedom." That's what it means.

I wag my tail when they feed me a big spaghetti dinner, and I laugh and play, but don't you dare think I don't know where I am ever second of every day. That gray background in my head makes sure I don't forget. And I dream prison dreams at night. I mean I even do time in my dreams.

So go fondle your tulips, Reader's Digest, and leave me alone.

My, what an outburst. But Reader's Digest? What got into you? (My do-gooder conscience weighing in.)

Fuck you. (My response.)

Okay, so maybe once in a while I wake up cross-eyed. But I get over it.

I started watering my little strip of weeds and grass again, mainly because it irritated old Simmons. And, sure enough, when he couldn't take it anymore, he pulled up on me. "Baker, why do you keep doing that?"

I shrugged. "I dunno. Something to do, I guess." He shook his head and walked away, headed over and talked to the captain who was duty officer that weekend and was checking out the yard at the time. I saw Simmons pointing at me as he talked and the captain was looking my way, so they must have been talking about me.

Well, here they came, the captain and Simmons, sidled up to me and stood there looking. Then the captain said, "How're you doing, Baker." He was talking to me. "Okay," I answered, and I think I had a shit-eating grin on my face, for I wasn't used to being asked that question by a captain in the middle of the yard in broad daylight, and I sort of liked the old fucker, anyway, so I didn't have my guard up.

He, the captain, studied that little raggedy patch of weeds, walked over next to the fence and looked closer, for the growth was pretty sparse, and he sort of bent down to look even closer, then he stood up straight and just stood there for a minute, then he turned to Simmons and said, "Leave it alone." That's what he said. And he walked away without another word. Just like that.

Simmons' face turned red, and he too went away, visibly shaken.

I watered the hell out of those weeds from then on.

And I remember that about that time I was studying my bridge book, preparing to challenge old Jackrabbit again, preparing to beat his smart ass, which turned out to be a disaster, for even though I studied till my face turned blue and pumped my nuts up until I walked like John Wayne, Jackrabbit again gave me a beating on that bridge table that hurt worse than the ass-whipping I took in the hole that day I got drunk, for he hurt my feelings.

Bastard!

Maybe spades was my game. Or marbles. I could shoot the hell out of marbles.

We got two showers a week at Alcatraz whether we needed them or not. I really didn't need a shower all that often, for I was young and fair-skinned and just naturally clean, but I took one just the same every shower day because that's the only place we got hot water, the shower room. And we had to take a shower to get clean clothes.

And besides, taking a shower was a good excuse to get out of my cell.

The evenings were long and boring. We had our earphones. That helped. Television was changing radio programs, but we still got Lux Radio Theatre, and Jack Benny and Amos and Andy and the Lone Ranger and Fibber Magee and Molly, and shows like that. And we got the ball games, we got those. And we got Lucky Lager Dance Time every night at ten o'clock—or was it nine-thirty? That was a music program sorta like a hit parade and I listened to it just about every night.

And we got the news. But all news programs were censored very closely by somebody out front, sort of like the magazines were censored: when any news came on about prison riots or bank-robbing or anything like that, the radio suddenly went dead, which always caused a hell of a commotion because when the radio went dead we got our tin cups and started banging on the bars, which did no good but we let them know we were there. Those tin cups banging on those steel bars made a racket you could hear all over the island. Somebody said that on a foggy night you could hear the banging all the way over in San Francisco, but I don't know whether I believe that or not.

Old Promising Paul made his rounds of the factory at least once a month, listening to complaints, mainly, and when he came in our shop half the workers gathered around him, mostly with desperate requests for a transfer somewhere else, anywhere else. Promising Paul had a little pad with him that he wrote complaints and requests on, he did that, and he promised everybody he'd see about it, but nothing ever came of it that I know of, for the same people gathered around him on every visit with the same woeful pleas, but nobody went anywhere.

Me, I didn't bother. I didn't have enough time left anyway. But Burgett did, and he was one of the people on the wailing wall every time the old warden came down.

I figured Burgett was working on a Plan B, though, with those air bags, that if a transfer didn't come through he'd try for a midnight parole. That's what I figured but I never asked him about it, for you didn't even dare whisper the word "escape" at Alcatraz for fear the snitches would hear it. Yes, we had snitches at Alcatraz, too. They had invisible antenna in their heads that constantly searched the air waves for plots that might be a ticket for a transfer. Anywhere you have desperate people you have snitches. And there were a lot of desperate people with a lot of serious time on Alcatraz Island.

Drake was one of those people. And he was a snitch, but we

didn't learn about him until it was too late. They finally caught up with him in Leavenworth and set his cell on fire with him in it. But that's another story. That's Roy Drake, not John Drake who was also at Alcatraz at the time. I don't want to hang a bad jacket on the wrong man.

When Promising Paul made his tours of the factory, he had a lot of shops to visit. On the waterfront, where I worked, was the glove shop and tailor shop and brush factory and, I think, a furniture factory down there somewhere, though I don't remember for sure for we were never allowed to see any of them unless we worked there. And on the landing going up the steps they had a laundry where they not only did convict's clothing but had a juicy contract with the military and with some hospitals, I think. All the shops had contracts with the military. And all of them made big money. The money they paid us didn't amount to much compared to what the factory made for Federal Prison Industries, which had factories in all the federal prisons. Jackrabbit told us this. He worked in the factory business office as a convict clerk, so he knew.

Me, I didn't care one way or the other because I didn't work anyway, just enough to get by. But we earned five days of extra goodtime a month for working there, so that was a good thing for anybody who ever expected to get out, which included me.

I had already lost all my statutory goodtime, which was the goodtime that was automatically awarded by law and was subtracted from your sentence by the record office when you first got to prison. You didn't have to earn that, but you could sure lose it quick. That was the catch.

The lazy summer puttered along. With September came the college football games on the radio, and then pro football, and finally the World Series in October. And with the World Series came our vacation, because we got off work to listen to the games on loud speakers on the yard, and if you listened or not it was extra yard time, which suited me just fine, the extra yard time. I had a ball.

I even won a game of bridge. Not from Jackrabbit, sadly, but I found a couple of beginners and beat the shit out of them, me and my partner. I don't even remember my partner's name but I do remember he was just as dumb as I was.

Jackrabbit didn't lose any money on the World Series because his precious Boston Red Socks were not in it, didn't even come close, therefore he couldn't bet on the bums that year, so he spent his vacation playing bridge and won money, uh, cigarettes, instead.

It was about that time that some convicts started betting their Christmas bags. Even though Christmas was still a long way off nobody was going anywhere, so it was legitimate to bet your bag early. Some people, like Russell, who had plenty of cigarettes, started buying up future Christmas bags as far as six months in advance, buying them up cheap as an investment, because the closer you got to Christmas the more they were worth and he could sell them after Christmas for twice what he paid for them. Others who worked in the factory bought bags early with factory money, with production tickets, for example. Like, if you worked in the glove shop, which was on piece-work, and you sewed a box of gloves, you had to initial a ticket proving you had sewn them. Well, if you made a deal with somebody who sold you a Christmas bag, you could let him initial the ticket and he'd get paid for it. That's the way some of them did it.

Me, I wasn't about to get rid of my bag for any amount of money. I was going to eat it, every bite of that sweet delicious candy, for we didn't get any candy at Alcatraz, except on Christmas. And though I hadn't yet spent a Christmas at Alcatraz, I had heard about the delicious contents of that Christmas bag described a thousand times. So, end of discussion.

Every once in a while I moseyed up on the concrete bleachers and checked out the paintings in progress by the convict artists. This one guy always got irritated when I stood peeping over his shoulder, so I stopped and peeped over his shoulder. Still the same painting, a big one of the whole panorama, the bay, the Golden Gate Bridge, the San Francisco waterfront, all in great detail that even included the tiny cars crossing the far-away bridge.

But there was something missing. So I kept looking, standing there with my hands in my pockets. So this guy had finally had enough, I guess, for he suddenly turned with his paint brush gripped tightly in his hand and his jaw clenched and said, "Why don't you go bother someone else. A painting is private and personal and I don't want you staring over my shoulder."

Well, I was a little surprised, I guess, and maybe a little off balance, but I still stood there without taking my hands out of my pockets, for I didn't feel threatened by his anger. And I finally said, "It ain't got any sea gulls in it."

"What!" His voice was about an octave higher.

"There's seagulls all over the sky out there and not a single one in your picture."

Well I thought he was going to strangle, and he very nearly did, I think. But he finally got control of himself and with a look of disgust on his face, he said, "There'll never be one of those nasty filthy things in this painting." Whereupon he seemed to think he'd won a point, I guess, because he went back to painting and ignored me. So I moseyed on, thinking about what he'd said.

Well, so help me I'm not making this up, I swear on my mother's honor, a few days later a miracle happened, the first of two that happened that October.

The first miracle blew my mind. I was walking the yard one day when I heard a blood-curdling scream come from up on the bleachers and when I looked I saw this artist who had been so put-out by my watching him paint. He was shaking his paint brush in the air. Then he had a genuine Alcatraz fit, kicked his painting, easel and all, so hard it bounced all the way down the bleachers and landed with a splat out on the yard. Then he slung his paint brush and all his paints after it, after which he continued cussing and shaking his fist in the air.

I knew what had happened, because I had heard that scream of disgust many times by now, though I had never heard it with so much anguish, maybe. But I had to see for myself. I moseyed over and looked down at his painting laying there, and sure enough, there was a big splat of seagull shit right in the middle of it with sickly streaks running in every direction. That seagull had dumped one hell of a load.

I know it was an accident and all, but, well, justice had been done.

The second miracle very nearly made a believer out of me. One weekend in late October when I went to the yard, the first thing I did was get me some water out of the faucet to water my raggedy weeds and when I got just about there I stopped suddenly and stared. My weeds had bloomed.

I mean it was just an ordinary day like any other day on Alcatraz Island, no angels singing, no trumpets in the background, and I don't believe in miracles anyway, but goddammit my weeds had bloomed. On a stack of bibles and my mother's honor, my sorry weeds had bloomed.

*****

CHAPTER SIX

Mama Nature was on the rag. Dark clouds rolled in from the west. Lightning flashed in jagged lines and thunder boomed. We were barely able to make it in off the yard before the rain came down in buckets, and even then, as last man in line I didn't entirely escape her wrath. Mama Nature could be a bitch sometimes.

The only thing that sort of saved the day was that the guards had to stay out till we were in so they got drenched too. And that included Simmons. He was sputtering and shaking himself off like a wet dog when he came in.

I don't mean to pick on Simmons, but he really had been on a roll lately, tearing up cells and writing petty disciplinary reports for everything. He nailed me one day for having my hair too long. Hair had to be cut smartly, well above the ears, and mine was just starting to get a little shaggy when he got me. I mean nothing ever came of it except I had to get a haircut, but it was his cocky attitude, like he had just busted me for attempted escape or something. That pissed me off. I kept my mouth shut, though.

And he caught Benny Rayburn masturbating in his cell one night when he was working the evening shift and actually wrote him up for it. I swear he did. We kidded Benny unmercifully about it, of course, because he was so easily embarrassed by things like that. And of course they threw the report away before it ever made it to court, so nothing ever came of that either, but Simmons didn't slow down a bit and many of his reports did stick. I mean he was a correctional officer at Alcatraz so they had to respect his uniform enough to process his most serious reports just to keep him happy. And like a traffic cop at a speed trap, he thrived on numbers: Write enough tickets and you'd get enough convictions to pay the rent, I guess that's the way Simmons looked at it.

As for Benny Rayburn, our pleasant-mannered jailhouse lawyer, he hadn't heard the end of it, yet, for Lieutenant Mitchell really rocked the boat the next day after dinner when we lined up to go back to work. We had no idea what was coming, of course. We lined up as usual in groups according to work detail, and Fat Mitchell and a couple of guards, serious as hell, walked down the lines looking everybody over. When the lieutenant got to Benny Rayburn he stopped, just stood there looking at Benny Rayburn for a minute, and then he moved on. When he got through with his inspection he took up a position in front of the whole gathering. "Benny Rayburn," he called out loud enough for everybody on the island to hear. And Benny, without any notion of what was coming, held up his hand and mumbled something.

Well Fat Mitchell asked, still serious and still loud enough to wake everybody up, "Are you able to work today?" Whereupon Benny, still puzzled, said, "Yes sir."

"Did you get through masturbating, yesterday?" Still serious as hell.

Well that was like dropping a hand grenade right in the middle of the crowd. At first everybody was sort of stunned that Fat Mitchell would say such a thing on the yard in front of everybody like that, then there were a few snickers, and then, man, we rolled on the ground with laughter while Benny Rayburn stood there turning twenty shades of red. And while you may not find this in the official history of Alcatraz, that really happened right there on Alcatraz Island just like that.

Anyway, back to Mother Nature's fit, I looked at old

Simmons standing there sputtering and fuming like a drowning dog and I turned my head quickly so he couldn't write me up for laughing in his face and I just about busted trying to hold it in. But the fun was about over because they locked us in our cells and that was it for the day. It was too late in the day for a rainy-day movie.

Most of the time I love Mother Nature. I love how she sometimes paints her blue sky with puffy white clouds that look like a stagecoach herding a flock of sheep, and how she decorates the land with trees and plants and flowers of every color in the rainbow, the endless variety of colors and shapes around every corner and over every hill, the simple truths and simple laws that even I can understand with which she keeps order in her kingdom. But she can be a bitch, sometimes, that's what I was thinking on that rainy day as I lay on my bunk with my wet clothes hanging over my fold-out desk and sulked, stuck in my cell for the rest of the day. I mean, Mother Nature, wise in all ways, nevertheless can't even tell the difference between real butter and Parkay margarine, the dumb bitch.

I'll give her credit for her art work, though, for I love this land called America, every inch of it, every hill and valley. I'd seen many miles of it before I was even sixteen years old, hitch-hiking around the country, setting pens in bowling alleys in Detroit, picking fruit with the Mexicans in California, up and down the highways I went wide open, and it didn't matter which direction I headed or how much money I had in my pocket, which was usually none, I loved every minute of it. We had no interstate highway system back then, only two-lane country roads when you got away from the cities, so around every turn and over every hill you saw a different sight, a one-of-a-kind painting you would never see again anywhere else, each one uniquely beautiful and constantly changing, and even if you took the same road back Mama Nature was there ahead of you, busy redecorating while you were gone.

The interstate highway system destroyed all that, of course, as I'm sure you've noticed as you cruise down Interstate-Whatever trying to stay awake from the sheer depressing monotony of a billion miles of the same scene repeated over and over again.

A painting on the wall may be a pretty sight, all right, but it's like a dead deer head, you have to kill it to paint it. My art is America, alive and changing every second, a deer running through the forest, dogwood trees blooming in the Spring, a thin trail of smoke coming from the stovepipe of a mountain cabin in the wintertime with white snow on the ground, the heat of summer when the girls come out of their clothes, a dog barking in the distance, Kathleen Vinson's pink panties hanging on a clothesline panting in the hot summer sun—what could be more American than that?

That painting on the wall might be worth a million dollars, a Picasso, a Rembrandt, but America was painted from sea to shining sea by the greatest artist of all, Mama Nature.

So, okay, I love my grandma and I love my dog and I love America. But that's it.

What? You don't think a thief can love his country? I've got news for you, I'd fight like hell to defend this country, except I am busy right now providing job security for a bunch of Alcatraz Island prison guards who don't seem to appreciate me the least bit. But many of America's biggest thieves served in the military with distinction and earned honorable discharges. Take the Hell's Angels, for example. As a group they are fiercely patriotic, and while they may steal the gold teeth right out of your mouth I've read of their fighting spirit in times of war, and I've witnessed their fighting spirit firsthand in prisons and jails where many of them wind up. On several occasions they volunteered for special military operations that required bravery and cunning far beyond the call of duty. The military didn't have the Navy Seals back then, I don't think, and dirty work had to be done. Well, let me tell you something, in later years I learned to admire and respect the heroic bravery of the Navy Seals, but when it comes to fierceness in battle, to pure meanness, they might not be too far ahead of the Hells Angels.

And did you know that almost every prison in the country has an official VFW chapter, the convicts? Yep, they do. Except for Alcatraz. We didn't have anything.

Nothing much happened the rest of my first year at Alcatraz until Christmas, nothing that I remember anyway. I don't remember who won the World Series or much about the football games except Y. A. Tittle and Hugh McElhenny were raising hell for the San Francisco Forty Niners, which many of us convicts considered our team. We didn't win the title but we beat the Los Angeles Rams, which was the main thing. The Baltimore Colts won everything, of course. They had Otto Graham.

And I remember I learned how to imitate the bawing of a fog horn on one of those tugboats that pestered us at night when it was foggy in the bay. I practiced it in my cell but never told anyone it was me, and never did it after the lights were out, for it's a part of our unwritten convict code that you never wake up a sleeping convict for anything unless the world's on fire.

I sure remember Christmas, though. On Christmas Eve day they called us in from work early and passed out our bags. When they were done all you could hear in the cell house was the rustling of paper sacks as prisoners tore into their precious bags, me included. I laid every item in my bag out on my bunk, salivating as I went, but I never ate a single thing until I had every item arranged and accounted for. I had a big bag of hard candy, that I would save till last and maybe start eating around February or March, maybe. And I had some candy bars I would eat right away, like right now, which I did, right then, for I could go no further. I chowed down.

Then somebody yelled out, "Three cheers for the Christmas bags!" And everybody yelled back, "Yea, yea, yea!" All at the same time, so it must have been a yearly tradition. And then somebody yelled out, "Three cheers for the guards who passed them out!" And everybody answered, "Shit, shit, shit!" And everybody laughed like hell. I had a hard time laughing with a mouth full of candy but I did.

When a couple of hours had passed and my stomach was stuffed, I carefully placed my big bag of hard candy on the shelf in back of my cell, and I vowed I wouldn't touch it again until January or February. Nope. And I opened up a fresh pack of Camels, which also had been in my bag, and I puffed away—that was back before cigarettes caused cancer, and a grown man would walk a mile for a Camel.

It was about that time that I heard one hell of a banging and clanging as the first of the check-ins started throwing all his belongings out of his cell and over the rail where they splattered and bounced on the cell house corridor below. Adding to the racket was the applause and yells of encouragement from other convicts. Yes, Alcatraz had its share of check-ins, those convicts who for one reason or another couldn't make it in regular population. Some just got bored with doing time and decided to take a break and check in the hole for a while to break up the monotony. Others checked in for their own protection, like those who got too far in debt and decided it was time to get out of town for a while. There were nearly always a few check-ins after a big ballgame, like the World Series or something. But the biggest number of check-ins came every year shortly after the Christmas bags were passed out, for many of the sorriest inmates had sold their Christmas bag to three or four different people, or lost it gambling to three or four different people, the same bag, so they just sat in their cells and ate up their bag as quickly as possible and then threw their belongings over the tier and waited for the guards to crack their door and take them to the hole, where they remained (in segregation) for things to cool down a bit.

Anyway, that was the traditional method of checking in at Alcatraz. And after Christmas, the cells in the hole filled up all the way.

And, yeah, in the late, rainless, Fall, my raggedy weeds died, despite my attention, no big deal, just part of Mother Nature's recycling operation, I guess, and the weeds didn't complain about it, they just turned brown and dropped dead, so I didn't make a big deal of it either, no burial ceremony or anything. I was still curious, though, about the flowers, because that had seemed like a miracle to me at the time. But Benny Rayburn told me a lot of weeds sprouted flowers, dandelions for example.

Shit, I always thought dandelions were flowers. So, oh well, maybe some people's weeds are another person's flowers. Because, me, I always did like dandelions. I used to admire them in the Spring, because they were among the first flowers to bloom, and I even picked a bunch of them when I was a kid and made a bouquet out of them, they were so yellow and beautiful. I proudly took them to school with intentions of presenting them to Kathleen Vinson, but before I got the chance she saw me coming and wrinkled up her nose at the sight of them, so I gave them to Miss Bell, the teacher, instead. I don't know what she, the teacher, did with them but she didn't put them in a vase on her desk where she usually put flowers her students brought her, and my grades didn't improve any, so I don't know.

Christmas Eve night I hung a sock on the bars for Santa Claus to fill up, a small act of silliness, I guess, to go with the Christmas spirit, and when I woke up the next morning my sock was empty, of course, but my heart and stomach were full. It's a good thing Reader's Digest didn't see the Christmas dinner they fed us that day or they'd have been screaming for our heads.

After Christmas, every time I came in from work that week I was greeted by the sight of that big bag of hard candy on my back shelf, but I vowed not to touch it until New Year's Eve and I didn't, except for a few small pieces just to sample it, maybe five or ten pieces, not many more.

New Year's Eve came and I still had almost half a bag of that delicious hard candy left, almost. After the lights were out many of us stayed up late to bring in the new year. Jackrabbit started a game of twenty-questions and we played on and on for a couple of hours, a bunch of supposed-to-be hardened convicts playing like a bunch of kids. It was a warm feeling between us that night that I remember so well for I felt a closeness to somebody that I hadn't felt since my grandma died. A lot of good people did time at Alcatraz.

I thought Burgett had given up on his plans with the air bags, but when we went back to work in January I saw him in the bathroom one day, again dunking a bag of air up and down in a bathroom sink filled with water. I must have earned his trust by then because he gave me a friendly greeting and asked me to watch for the boss for a little while. Which I did.

*****

CHAPTER SEVEN

Forest Tucker was walking the yard with Roy Drake, both hunched forward like humpbacked turtles against the winter wind. And both were talking with a good deal of excitement, so I knew they were talking about robbing banks. That's what Forest Tucker liked to talk about. I might have joined them but I'd heard their stories so many times I decided against it, and, besides, I didn't like Roy Drake all that much, anyway. There was something sneaky about him. He liked to talk about how he moved into this little town in Arkansas and opened a little business of some kind as a front, and then proceeded to make friends with the local businessmen, joined the Chamber of Commerce, buddied up to a local bank official until he learned the routine at the bank, and then he robbed that bank, took all the money and split. I don't see anything wrong with robbing a bank, but to make friends with a man and then rob him, there's something wrong with that. And so I walked alone, thinking some serious thoughts.

I remember that scene very well because that was the day I decided I'd had enough of prison life. I decided I needed to learn a trade. That's what I decided.

They had a lot of bank robbers at Alcatraz, and most of them had a wheelbarrow load of time. Twenty-five years, fifty years—federal judges in those days had a lot of time to give and not enough people to give it to, so I guess they had to give it to somebody. That's what I figured. Therefore, I decided I didn't want to be a bank robber.

So when I saw old Courtney Taylor all alone over in the corner of the wall nearest to the card tables, where the wind didn't seem to be blowing as much, which was a good sign, in my mind, that he was smarter than a bank robber, for at least he had sense enough to get somewhere out of the wind. I cut across the yard and approached him. He was a portly man — sort of fat but not obese, so I guess that's portly — I approached him and asked him if he'd teach me how to make counterfeit checks. We already knew each other well enough for me to ask him that question, and he agreed without hesitation, for he was the best check-man in the world and never missed a chance to talk about it.

He told me about transit numbers and routing numbers and account numbers and bank logos and company logos, he talked till my head got dizzy. And I didn't learn a thing that first day except that Courtney Taylor was a downright genius, but in the weekends that followed, his teachings started to sink in and I slowly absorbed every word he said. So that winter in Alcatraz I learned a trade.

I was talking to Benny Rayburn about it one day, for by then his likable manner had earned my trust. In fact we had already decided to invite him to play on our raggedy softball team in the coming season. I mean, jailhouse lawyer or not, anybody stupid enough to let old Simmons catch him jacking off in his cell was worthy of being a Gullie. Anyway, I was talking to him about all the good stuff I was learning from Courtney Taylor and he listened for a while, but then he just had to interrupt.

"He's in here," he said.

"Huh?" I said.

"He's in here," he repeated.

"What?" I said.

"He got caught, just like the rest of us. Everyone in here got caught. These are the wrong people to learn from, don't you think?"

Smartass Benny Rayburn.

Actually, Benny Rayburn's last name was spelled with a "born," Rayborn, instead of a "burn," but we called him Benny Rayburn, using the whole name, because it had a lyrical quality to it which better matched his personality, maybe, I don't know, that's just what we called him, and the only reason I mention it here is so if you decide to Google him in *Federal Defenders of San Diego, about Ben Rayborn,* you'll spell his name right and you'll find out that he was considered by J. Edgar Hoover to be the most dangerous gangster to come out of World War Two, which shows you how paranoid old J. Edgar was and also how wrong, for Benny Rayborn was probably the least dangerous man I've ever known. But he was the most remarkable.

At age twenty-one Benny Rayburn was the leader of a gang of bank robbers who called themselves the Benny-Denny Gang and he received a life sentence in the state of Kentucky where he led a prison riot in protest of the inhumane conditions there. For that he was sent to Alcatraz. That isn't the remarkable part. When he got to Alcatraz he got a job in the prison library and started reading every law book he could find.

Well, Benny Rayburn had an unusual mind in that he could understand the gibberish in law books and translate it into plain language in such a clear and reasonable way that before long he was writing briefs and writs and all that tricky stuff for fellow prisoners at Alcatraz. He was getting results, too.

Eventually, because of his ability to understand and translate what he had read, he got his own sentences reduced, both his life sentence in Kentucky and a Federal sentence related to the same crime, and he was set free.

However, his freedom didn't last long. He was convicted in Tennessee. Again for bank robbery. While serving his time in Tennessee he continued to file briefs and writs and such for inmates there. And while there he also started a class in Constitutional Law, teaching other inmates. His work in law was so brilliant that he attracted the attention of John Cleary, a professor of law at Emory University and head of an advocacy group which helped prisoners with post-conviction relief. He was so impressed with Benny Rayburn's work that he convinced state authorities to release him into his custody after Benny got his state sentence in Tennessee cut in half.

Again Benny Rayburn was free. This time, though, he went to work for John Cleary's law group and followed the group to San Diego when they opened the Federal Defender office there. And for the next thirty years Benny Rayburn worked for that group as Chief Legal Research Associate, training new lawyers in the practical aspects of law, himself filing thousands of briefs all the way from the local level to the Supreme Court of the United States of America. All this without a single day of law school. That's what's remarkable.

Me, I didn't know anything about the law except how to break it.

He tried to tell me some things about law a few times, just talking. I remember one time he told me that a law book doesn't necessarily mean what it says, that it means what the judge says it says. I remember that. And I remember thinking that a law book must be sort of like the bible, that the bible says what the preacher says it says.

Benny Rayburn worked in the prison library at Alcatraz for a long time, but now he was working out front somewhere as a clerk for the warden and his bunch. As a result he was able to pick up a little information here and there and start some pretty potent rumors. One rumor was that funds were approved for the purchase of a big walk-through metal detector, which they planned to install somewhere between the yard and the factory. Jackrabbit came up with a bigger rumor than that. He heard, from his position as a clerk in the factory business office, that there was a lieutenant pushing for building a fence across the concrete bleachers on the yard so you could only go up so high and therefore couldn't see over the wall. He claimed that such a fence would be good for security reasons because if you couldn't see the free world by looking over the wall you would be less tempted to want to escape, that the sight of the world was a temptation that could be eliminated by such a fence.

Well, we declared Jackrabbit to be the winner for the worst rumor, for we couldn't think of anything more terrible than not being able to look out over the wall.

Prison guards earn brownie points and promotions for new ideas on how to make prisons more secure, not only from the standpoint of preventing escapes but mainly for better control of the inmate population, better control with less work, of course. Guards don't earn points on suggestions like better food and education and recreation and nonsense like that.

In the federal prison system the captain is responsible for the daily operation of the prison. His office schedules the work hours of the guards, days off, vacations, things like that. He is also responsible for security. All ideas involving security issues or anything that might become a security issue has to cross his desk for approval. So the captain is all powerful when it comes to passing out brownie points. But the captain has to go to the warden for his own brownie points.

The warden is king. And when he steps into his kingdom people start trembling: staff, guards, inmates, dogs, cats, everything. And at Alcatraz the warden was more powerful than God. He, the warden, had the power of life and death and he could terminate your existence on Earth whether it was your time to go or not. Not that he walked around terminating people, but you knew without a doubt that he could. You could tell. Just the way he walked.

A prison warden is two foot taller than everybody else, but I think that's because people shrink a couple of feet in his awesome presence and that he's just taller by comparison. That's what I figure.

I've noticed over the years one peculiarity that all wardens have in common. They have a compulsion to build a fence. I think it's in their genes. I mean, whenever a new warden takes over a prison, the first thing he does, it seems to me, is survey his little kingdom to figure out where to build a fence, *his* fence. There may be fences all over the place, and I don't mean fences around the prison to keep people from escaping, I mean fences inside the prison, a fence around the yard, two fences around the yard, a fence between two buildings, another fence around the yard, forever and ever. I've seen a warden tear down a perfectly good fence just so he could build one of his own. And if you think I'm making this up just go look at USP Leavenworth today. It has a huge sixty-foot wall around it that few have successfully climbed over, and I'll be dammed if some warden didn't build a fence all the way around the outside of the wall. Look inside the prison out on the yard and you'll see another fence *inside* the wall. Then look around you and you'll see fences in every direction, so many that you can hardly walk fifty feet without bumping into one.

There were so many fences in Leavenworth at one time that one warden just threw up his hands and painted the wall purple. Figure that out.

But back to Alcatraz in the winter of fifty-seven/fifty-eight, old Benny Rayburn walked up to me one day all friendly-like and asked me what color my cell was. He was always thinking up some weird question or riddle or something, so when he asked me that stupid question I knew he was up to something. But I'll be dammed, I couldn't answer because I really hadn't noticed what color my cell was, exactly, I mean I hadn't ever really thought about it, but the best I could remember at that exact time was that it was some kind of shitty gray color, so I answered, "Gray."

He just sort of smiled and said, "Nope. Gray is the color of your mind." And he went on about his business without any explanation. Caught somebody else with it, then somebody else. He really had a fly up his nose.

Messed my head up. Like I said, Benny Rayburn could sure be a smartass sometimes. What a stupid question, but I couldn't wait to get back to my cell and see. And what I saw messed my head up even more, for it wasn't gray, it was sort of a dirty two-tone color, the walls, with so much nicotine stain from cigarette smoke, well, it could have been gray. I wasn't about to wash the walls to find out.

Gray is the color of your mind.

Bullshit. Not *me!*

I decided it was time to stir up some shit again. Maybe make some more home brew, only this time I would do the counting myself and leave it set for ten days. Well, maybe five days. Or maybe I could think of something to do to Simmons. He was tearing up cells again.

As it turned out Mama Nature gave me a whole new idea, for the fog rolled in that night and the tugboats started chugging and the foghorns started bawing and opportunity knocked on my head.

I got out of bed and started answering the foghorns, imitating their sound with my mouth and hands, as I had previously learned to do. Since each horn had a different pitch, I was even able to imitate that. But then I decided I'd make my own pitch, different from any of those out in the bay. And I chose a lowdown ghostly sound that was so real it sent chills down my own spine.

I violated the convict code of never wake up a sleeping convict, all right, but it was time for a wake-up call on Alcatraz Island and it was up to me to do it. So I did it. At first there were sleepy grumbles from the cells, then louder protests as more people woke up. Amid all this somebody said, "Sounds like there's a foghorn in the cell house! Hear that sound?" And somebody else said, "Sounds like it's coming from upstairs." Then somebody else said, "Naw, it sounds like it's coming from the ceiling. Sounds like a ghost!"

Whitey Knight, my next door neighbor was very superstitious. He called out my name and asked me if I heard it. So I said, "Yes," and added, "It sounds like it's coming out of the pipe corridor behind the cells. It sounds like a ghost to me too." When I said that, Whitey cleared his throat as was his habit when he got nervous, and I heard him walking his cell. There were rumors that Alcatraz was haunted, anyway, so who was I to spoil a good rumor. I mean Alcatraz was once an old military prison and it was rumored to have dungeons and more dungeons below our cells that we never saw but we heard about them all the time, rats and water dripping and that kind of stuff. And ghosts.

So I kept up my ghostly bawing and it began to sound like the foghorns out in the bay were answering *me!* It was like a witches' convention had gathered around the island.

Well that did it. Everybody was awake now, a party in the making. At first there was one tin cup banging on the bars, then another, and then all hell broke loose, whooping and hollering and banging. Stuff started sailing over the range and then the smell of smoke came from every direction as people started setting things on fire and tossing out blazing paper airplanes and things like that.

Off-duty guards and the goon squad were called in quickly, but it was too late. Alcatraz wouldn't sleep that night, and that included the whole island, guards, women and children, cats and dogs, everything.

They arrested about a half-dozen people, those who they caught in the act of setting fires or getting a little too wild, like one guy busted his toilet bowl off the wall and started a hell of a flood, but otherwise they didn't mess with anybody, just let them holler and bang till they got tired, and by daylight it was all over. That's the way they did things at Alcatraz. The old warden didn't believe in mass punishment, they only arrested those who were caught in the act. And then the next morning they cracked the doors and everybody went to chow and they blew work-call and everybody went to work just like nothing had happened. In any other prison they would have locked the whole place down for days, maybe weeks.

The only thing they did was while we were at work they tore up our cells and threw a lot of our stuff out. They did that. And they weren't nice about it. When I came in from work that day, all sleepy-eyed and tired, all I had left in my cell was standard issue, and that was on the floor.

But we expected that. And time went on. But the color of our minds were not gray anymore for a while, thanks to Benny Rayburn.

One day I went in from work and found a library book on my bed. Instead of being a Zane Grey book, as usual, it was a raggedy old science book that I'd had on my list forever. So I plopped down on my bunk and consumed it, one painful word after another. It had a lot of stuff in it about space and time and inertial frames and Einstein and Newton and a guy named Galileo, and I walked around with a sprained brain for weeks as I read it over and over trying to figure it out. And when it was due back in the library I didn't send it back, and I got a dirty note from the librarian and I still didn't send it back, I hid it under my mattress, and then one day I came in and the book was gone. So I guess the old librarian had come and shook my cell down and found it, and I guess he was pissed off for he left my cell all tore up. That's what they do if they're pissed off, leave your cell all tore up.

I lost my library privileges for a month, but that's all right because I had it all floating around in my brain somewhere, all those great people and all the great things they said. Einstein: "The laws of nature must be the same in all inertial frames." Hot damn! And Newton: "A body in motion tends to remain in motion." And Galileo: "In the cabin of a ship moving at constant velocity, water drips straight down, a ball bounces equally in any direction—you don't notice the motion of the ship because you are a part of that motion." All three great men talking about the same thing in different words leading to a conclusion that neither space nor time is absolute, that, uh, never mind, it was all washing around up there in my brain but it hadn't quite washed up on the same shore.

Well I had no one to discuss it with and I hated to suffer a sprained brain alone so I decided to try it out on Benny Rayburn. I talked, explaining what great stuff I'd learned, and he listened, but his eyes kept darting here and there. When I was just getting to the good part, he suddenly spotted somebody and just as suddenly excused himself saying he had to get some information from this guy to file a motion for him that was suddenly due the next day. And he took off.

Well, okay. I found Burgett doing pushups and tried it out on him when he came up for air. I mean, what are friends for? He listened for a few minutes with a stone face. Then he said. "Fuck you, Bill Baker," and he walked away. I guess he was through doing push-ups for the day.

Okay. I wasn't about to give up, though. I sought out Forest Tucker. Started explaining it to him. He would listen. He was a true friend. And he did listen, politely, looking me straight in the eye as true friends do. And when I was through, he said, "You need to come to band practice, Bill Baker. I need your help." That's what he said.

He sat there all that time, he did, listening politely as a sad dog, didn't yawn once, well maybe his eyes glazed over a few times, and maybe he squirmed a few times, but he listened. And when I was done he sat silently until he was sure I was done and then he said, "You need to come to band practice, Bill Baker. I need your help." That's all he said. And he looked so pitiful and I felt so guilty because I had been skipping practice for a long time, that I said I would.

And I could have kicked my own ass afterward, for I knew why he needed me. He had a guitar player already who could read music and everything, he just couldn't make it through any song without getting his timing turned around, and once he did that he couldn't ever get straightened out because he didn't know he was turned around. He was rhythm deaf. He had no natural sense of timing.

Me, I had a natural gift, both in timing and pitch. My only problem was that I couldn't read music. So I guess old Forest

Tucker figured that if he had one guitar player with perfect rhythm and another who could read music, he'd have himself a guitar player.

Life just wasn't fair.

*****

CHAPTER EIGHT

Simco was out of the hole. He was back on the yard and everybody was aware of it. Anybody else might have gone unnoticed, but not Simco. He was a coldblooded killer.

It wasn't that he invited anybody's notice, he didn't. He was quiet, polite, and if you didn't know better you'd swear he was recently graduated from some Ivy League college, maybe Yale, and then you might guess he'd gone on to serve his country for a few years, maybe as a fighter pilot. Clean-cut, handsome, with a good smooth jaw, you might want to introduce him to your daughter, do a little match-making, for he must have great genes. And he had those eyes, calm, non-offensive. Might be a marine, no, not enough fire in those eyes. The calm before the storm? Maybe. A cat ready to pounce? Absolutely not, for he was too relaxed, too sure of himself to bother with such aggressive games.

But then when he took his shirt off and you saw his smooth skin and slim, hard-packed waist and hard muscled body, well, something didn't add up.

He had killed his punk. I don't know why, I'm just telling you what I know. He killed his punk, his sissy, whatever you want to call him. He killed him in cold blood down in the shower room with a guard looking straight at him. He stood over his punk and calmly watched him die while the guard threw a roll of toilet paper at him from a distance trying to break it up. That's the truth, threw a roll of toilet paper at him, which as far as I'm concerned was a brave act, for I wouldn't even have done that. I'd have got the hell out of there as soon as I heard the sound of that knife thudding into flesh. The killing thrust of a knife is not silent. It has a distinct thud, and if you ever hear it you'll remember it forever. Simco killed his punk right there in broad daylight in front of a guard who committed the brave act beyond the call of duty of throwing a roll of toilet paper at him.

And then Simco calmly and voluntarily allowed them—for in short order there were a whole gang of guards present, all out of breath and none willing to get close to that bloody knife—Simco allowed them to take him to the hole where he remained for many months until he went to court over in San Francisco and was found not guilty by a jury, not guilty of anything because the jury of ordinary people couldn't believe for one minute that such a nice, clean-cut boy imprisoned at Alcatraz with all those monsters could possibly be guilty of murder and if he was he must have done it in self-defense to keep from being raped or mutilated or maybe even eaten alive.

The citizens of San Francisco knew that the prisoners at Alcatraz were the most terrible creatures in the world. They knew because they were told so by glowing accounts in newspapers and radio and now even television. And of course the politicians and tour boat captains and everybody else who had never set foot on Alcatraz Island fanned the flames with wild rumors and ghost stories which reinforced what the public already believed. "So what was Simco doing at Alcatraz, anyway. The government must have made a mistake."

And when Simco's lawyer requested that Simco remove his shirt in the courtroom to prove a point, the point being forgotten when the ladies in the jury witnessed Simco's hard young body—

Not guilty.

This, despite graphic testimony by the guard who had been an eye witness to the whole thing. I don't know if the roll of toilet paper was introduced into evidence or not.

And Simco's case was not the only one thrown out by a disbelieving jury. A big Iowa boy with a baby face (or was it Teexas?) strangled a guy to death while I was there. Again, the jury would not believe it was unjustified. Not guilty.

You had to kill a prison guard to be found guilty by a San Francisco jury. Then it was automatic.

Me, I knew both Simco and the other guy—though I can't remember the Iowa boy's name—and it was okay with me that they beat their cases. The guys they killed were not monsters, but neither were they pillars of prison society. And in prison when a murder happens it's usually as much the fault of the victim as it is the guy who killed him.

Anyway, Simco, after being acquitted of the murder charge, still had to deal with prison authorities, and they didn't care what the jury said, they kept him in the hole for many more months before they finally put him back in population. And now Simco was on the yard again.

Simco spelled his name Simcox, But it sounded like Simco so that's how I'm spelling it. I mean you don't walk around asking a cold blooded killer how to spell his last name. Not at Alcatraz you don't.

He was really cool, though. I only saw him lose his composure one time, and that was up in the hospital one night. They checked me in overnight because I had a tooth pulled that day and it wouldn't stop bleeding. Simco was also there for some minor reason, as were several other guys. We were all together in a little hospital ward containing maybe a half-dozen beds, but to get to the shower you had to cross the main hospital hallway. Well, Simco went across to take a shower and when he came back he was upset. He said Stroud (Birdman), who was in a special, solotary cell over that way, had hit on him for sex. But what he, Simco, was upset about was, in his own words, "Birdman hit on me to suck my dick, and I told the fucker, 'You don't hit on me, I'm the one who does the hitting, if I want my dick sucked I'll hit on *you!*'" And he, Simco, said it quite loudly right there in the hospital ward for everybody to hear.

Messed my head up when I heard that. Simco was upset because he was a pitcher, not a catcher, and he left no doubt how he felt about it. He was the man, the hitter not the hittee. I almost laughed because it sounded so ridiculous. I believe his feelings were hurt.

But I was surprised, too, because Robert Stroud was a hero, a genuine bonafide hero. He had written the book about diseases in birds. He was the worldwide authority. After many painstaking years of study in a solitary cell in Leavenworth with real live birds, he had written the book. And he had endured most of his life in a solitary cell and still had life to go, and that alone was a heroic accomplishment in my opinion, never mind the birds.

Everybody took showers, so I figured I'd better take one too whether I needed one or not. I got into my bathrobe and headed that way, sort of sneaked across the hall trying to avoid Birdman's cell. But from a cell up the hall he called to me. He saw me and I saw him, and for a moment I stopped. What I saw in that brief moment was a dark cell with a gray shadow of a man peering out at me with bright white eyes streaked with red coal fires of hell, and I got no further. I turned around and got the heck away from there.

I didn't take a shower. Like I said, I was young and just naturally clean. I vowed to take more showers when I got to be a dirty old man, if I ever made it that far. But right then, at that moment, I wasn't in any mood to take a shower. I hit my bunk and did some serious thinking.

Without going into detail about my roundabout reasoning, I came to several conclusions about what I'd seen and heard that evening. 1. Homosexuals could be heroes too, no getting around it. 2. I was in favor of capital punishment, provided it was carried out quickly. To sentence a man, no matter what his crime, to life in solitary confinement was wrong, no getting around that either, because there must come a time in the life of any prisoner serving such a sentence when the punishment far outweighs the severity of whatever crime he committed. And when that happens he is no longer responsible for the crime but is the victim instead. And when I saw the remains of Robert Stroud, Birdman, in that dark cell, that gray shadow with those bright white eyes streaked with the red coal fires of hell, I knew I was looking at the victim.

Many years before, when Birdman was serving time in Leavenworth, according to a guy I met later who was there and saw what happened, he, Robert Stroud, had a punk. They bunked together, ate their meals together and did whatever they did together. Well, this one guard kept messing with them in the mess hall when they went to eat. Maybe he didn't like homosexuals, I don't know, but he kept messing with Stroud and his punk every time they went to eat, so Stroud finally got tired of the whole thing and killed him, the guard. And that was that.

I'm not saying the killing was justified. Killing a guard is a serious matter, whether he needs killing or not, and while I might cuss one out or maybe put up a fight I sure wouldn't think of killing one, no matter how sorry he was. But Robert Stroud was homicidal. And a homicidal homosexual is the most dangerous animal in the world. So Robert Stroud did what he did because he was who he was.

At that point if they had taken him to the hole and beat him to death, I would say, okay, call it even, an eye for an eye. He did what he did and they did what they did and that's the end of the story. But they had to have more than that. They wanted his soul. They buried him alive.

But the soul is a hard thing to kill, I guess. Birdman wrote the book on birds and here he was, still alive. After all that time in solitary confinement it's a wonder he wasn't eating his own shit, so if he was still sane enough to suck a dick, more power to him, as long as he didn't mess with mine.

History will even things out, anyway. It always does. Birdman will not only be a hero but he'll be a martyr. The judge who sentenced him to life in solitary confinement will be the villain, as will the prison guards and the warden and the whole criminal justice system of the time.

To be fair and accurate, Birdman was at first sentenced to death for killing that guard, but he received a commutation to life by President Wilson and was then ordered to spend the rest of his life in solitary confinement.

Birdman eventually died in the Medical Center for Federal Prisoners at Springfield, Missouri. He was still in solitary confinement when he died. So they got every ounce of flesh out of him they could, but they still didn't get his soul.

And History will have the last word.

I survived my ordeal with the dentist, which may have been a miracle, because somebody said he was a horse doctor over in San Francisco. He only worked part-time at Alcatraz, a contract worker or something like that. Anyway I got out of the hospital and hit the yard that weekend as usual, and I skipped band practice. Forest Tucker surely wouldn't blame me after what I'd been through with that horse-doctor dentist. And it was such a beautiful day.

Me and Burgett and Jackrabbit sat up high on the bleachers so we could see. Jackrabbit wasn't playing bridge that day because his beloved Boston Red Sox were playing and the game was being broadcast over the loud speakers up on the wall. The Red Sox were losing, as usual, but that didn't matter, Jackrabbit loved them just the same.

The sky was high and blue. Sea gulls sailed on spread wings in search of who knows what. It was that kind of day. I remember it well because that was the day the girl in a bikini came into my life.

Small sail boats speckled the bay with their white sails blowing in the wind. Speed boats towed water skiers here and there. And here came the Alcatraz tour boat, right on schedule. They could only come so close to the Island, though, and there was a guard in the tall tower above the factory who had a bull horn to warn them away if they got too close and a high-powered rifle just in case they didn't listen. The tour boat stopped and I could hear the loud speakers. I couldn't hear exactly what they were saying, the loud speakers, but it would be the usual tourist stuff: Al Capone, Machine Gun Kelly, the escape attempts, and of course the monster stories and ghost stories, anything to excite the passengers. And I imagine they had a big DON'T FEED THE ANIMALS sign on the boat somewhere.

The boat finally left.

We weren't talking much, me and Burgett and Jackrabbit, just soaking up some springtime sun. The artists were up there, too, with their easels, painting freedom. And I was leaning back watching the seagulls in their lazy travels, some venturing higher than others or farther out toward the open sea, the adventurous ones, maybe preparing their genes for the coming of the Chosen One. I didn't know anything about Jonathon Livingston Seagull at the time, of course, because the book hadn't yet been written, but I could tell something was up, that some gulls were more daring than others, and I could imagine that someday one brave bird would break free from the flock and sail away on a great adventure and might never return. I remember thinking that.

From the corner of my eye I saw Burgett suddenly straighten up, saw his back stiffen. At first I thought a fly ball might be heading our way, but then he stood up and hollered my name and pointed excitedly toward something in the bay. So I jumped up, too.

And there she was, a girl in a bikini on water skis heading straight for Alcatraz, and getting closer every second. Damn! Closer and closer she came, causing the tower guard to take quick action. First he bellowed on the bull horn for her to stop, even though it was obvious that she wasn't going to, that the speedboat wasn't going to, though I wasn't paying any attention to the speed boat. The guard lowered his rifle and hollered into his bull horn again, this time in a high-pitched voice, then he picked up his rifle again, aimed it.

At the last possible second the speedboat turned sharply away. The girl in the bikini was on a long tow rope, so when the boat turned it slung her in a long wide arc that sent her even closer to the shore. She was so close we could plainly hear her high-pitched laughter, for she was having a real thrill, no doubt about it. The guard pointed his rifle again as she reached the closest point of her arc, but he couldn't pull the trigger, I guess. Instead he screamed into his bullhorn again.

Then the speed boat sped away taking her with it. She shook her red bikinied butt as she skied away, swerving this way and that.

She wasn't through though. Here she came back. This time she came closer, daringly. And by now half the prisoners on the yard were up on the bleachers yelling at the top of their lungs, cheering her on. And on she came. The guard couldn't stand it anymore. He let out a scream and then he picked up his rifle and fired it into the air.

And again the speed boat swerved and slung the girl in a wide circle which brought her dangerously close to shore. Long hair flying, she was laughing still. Man, she was beautiful. And she wasn't no mermaid, either, for she had long white legs to go with her slim shapely body. She laughed and waved as she swung close, then she was gone, her round butt bobbing sadly as she left.

And I was in love with her for days afterward.

*****

CHAPTER NINE

How did I wind up in Alcatraz? Good question. But I don't know; must have been something I did.

Let's see, when I got out of the state prison in Salem, Oregon, I walked down to the bus station, well I sort of bounced down there for my legs were on springs of happiness. I mean getting out of prison is the best feeling in the whole world, and if I had died that day I know I'd have gone straight to heaven because I know the heavenly angels would have scooped me up as one of their own so full of joy was I, and old Saint Peter would have waved me right in without even asking for ID. That's how happy I was.

My old step dad had set me free when I was sixteen, so I didn't have any place to go, but I had twenty-five bucks of gate money in my pocket and the clothes on my back and that's all I needed. I went where most other ex-convicts went who didn't have anywhere else to go. I went to Portland, and once I got there I went again to where a lot of ex-convicts went, I went to Denty Moore's Tavern downtown.

Denty Moore's tavern had a little restaurant in the back part of it where I sat down and ordered the house special, which was a bowl of Denty Moore's beef stew right fresh out of a can. I didn't order a beer right then because I was so high on getting out of prison that I was afraid a beer would make me sober. I ordered a glass of milk. And I guess my trip to Alcatraz started right there, not that the glass of milk had anything to do with it, but it so happened that the guy who ran the restaurant was a small-time fence for stolen goods and I fell right in with his program, ready and willing and the sooner the better, for the twenty-five bucks I had started out with was already half gone.

But first there was this pretty young blonde hanging out with some guys, one of which I knew from prison, and I think they steered her my way, knowing I'd just got out. I had a good reputation in state prison and a lot of respect. Anyway the girl's name was Signey Meeker. Her husband was in the county jail out at Rocky Butte and her boyfriend was in the city jail downtown, so she was on the loose. With a beer in her hand she came right over to my table and introduced herself, friendly as heck. And that night she took me to her apartment and relieved me of my burden. And when I next saw the sweet warm sunlight I cast a taller shadow on the land.

Signey Meeker was a happy girl, just wanted to have fun, so I buddied up with her. Together we broke in to some cigarette distributer buildings around Portland, because that's what the fence wanted most, cigarettes. She was eighteen, I was twenty-two, and for both of us there was no tomorrow. We were wide open, moving so fast that we must have lived a hundred years in the couple months of Earth-time we were together, taking into consideration Relativity and the speed of light and all that.

And then one night I got busted and then Signey Meeker had a husband in Rocky Butte and two boyfriends in the city jail. And that's the last I saw of her.

I didn't stay in jail very long, though, not that time. I noticed that they sort of left the door open when they brought in the chow cart to feed us, and the office guard was doing his morning routine in the kitchen feeding his own face, so I hid behind the lock-box and when they opened the grill, away I went, full blast, down the hallway, into the office and down the elevator.

I hid until dark and then stole a car, hot-wired it like I'd been taught in prison, which was easy because car ignitions only had two or three wires in those days. I drove through the night, crossed the long bridge across the Columbia River into Washington State, where I took side roads till I came to a good place to hide until daylight. I was just about out of gas and would have to figure out how to get some before I went much further.

Having been up all night on the run, and all pumped up on adrenalin, I stayed awake counting my blessings, so far so good considering I didn't know how to drive. I had never driven an automobile before that night. But they say God watches over idiots.

I waited until well past daylight until I started the car, not wanting to waste gasoline. I cruised down a few farm roads until I spotted a farm house with a big gas tank out by an old wooden shed. I pulled into the yard and knocked on the door of the house, waited, knocked again. No answer. My luck was holding out. I drove back to the shed, got out, looked for the gas cap on the car, couldn't find it, went around and around the car, still couldn't find it. Wasting time!

Then I spotted a five-gallon gas can setting beside the tank. I grabbed it and filled it up, set it in the car. I got in and took off. Got out of there and down the road. Pulled off behind some trees. Got out and looked for the gas cap, around and around I went, still couldn't find it. The fucking car didn't have a gas cap! Damn!

I dropped down on my belly and looked under the car. It had a gas tank, near the rear. I scooted back there real quick, dropped down and looked underneath again, found the metal hose that went into the tank. Logical. Traced it to…somewhere behind the license plate. Yes, somewhere behind the license plate. I stood up, looked at the license plate. It would have to come off.

No tools. Wasting time. I ran around to the glove

compartment, found a screwdriver. I unscrewed the screws in the license plate, took the plate off. Nothing but a frame there. Damn!

I examined the frame, beat on it, tugged on it. Suddenly while I was tugging the frame came down, opened up. It was on some kind of hinge with a spring. And there was the gas cap. I'll be damn. I looked around me instinctively to see if anybody saw how stupid I was. I grinned, blushed probably, laughed, what a fucking idiot! But I had solved the gas cap riddle and I hurried and screwed the plate back on the frame and poured the gas out of the can and into the tank. And away I went.

I came to a main two-lane highway and turned right. Driving was fun. On-the-job training. More fun than playing in the dirt with toy cars. This was the real thing. I looked for the knobs for the radio.

The engine started making a noise, just a little knock at first, then louder. Then it started bucking like a wild horse. Smoke started pouring out of the back, dark black smoke. I slowed down, but when the engine sounded like it was about to stall, I gunned it and it sounded better. So I went barreling down the highway at seventy miles an hour, bucking and jerking and laying down a dark black smoke screen. All I could do was hang on and hope I could find a place to stop, but no such place was in sight. Other cars swerved to get out of my way. I was gripping the steering wheel with white knuckles, hanging on to a charging automobile that had suddenly gone mad.

Thankfully I came to a little town and turned off on the first side-street I came to. And as soon as I did that the engine stopped. So I let it roll down a little hill and pulled over and stopped in front of a little church. I tried several times to start it again, but nothing happened. It was dead.

I got out and raised the hood, stood looking at the engine. Not that I could do anything about it, I didn't know a thing about cars, but I didn't know what else to do, so I stood there and looked hopelessly. I mean I hated to leave it. It was my first car.

After a while a fellow came out of the church and asked me if I was having trouble with my car, so I explained how it had acted going down the road, bucking and smoking and all that, and he walked around the car, flipped down the license plate like it wasn't nothing, removed the gas cap and sniffed, put the gas cap back on. When he came back he said it smelled like diesel fuel, that diesel fuel would make a car act like what I had described.

Well I just stood there, dumbstruck, realizing what I had done, and I said damn, I must have used the wrong pump at the gas station when I filled it up. He gave me a strange look and said I'd better call a wrecker because that car wasn't going any further. And then he walked on down the street, left me standing there looking pitiful. I guess my luck had run out.

So to make a sad story short, that night I slept in an old truck, and the next morning just before daylight I went looking for a drink of water. Mistake number ninety-nine. A cop saw me and arrested me on suspicion and hauled me off to jail. Within twenty-four hours they had me identified, within thirty days I was sentenced in federal court to four years in prison for transportation of a stolen car across a state line, and a week after that I was sitting in a cell in the United States Penitentiary at McNeil Island, Washington. Justice was swift in those days. You are who you are, you did what you did and, bang, next case.

So I guess that was the second step on my road to Alcatraz. Third step coming up.

McNeil Island wasn't too bad. The food was okay and the prison was wide open. You could go anywhere you wanted any time of day and do whatever you wanted to do, as long as you didn't try to climb over their raggedy fence, which was the first thing I vowed to do as soon as I could figure out a way to cross the water to the mainland. In the meantime, while I was figuring, they must have been figuring, too, must have got my record from the state prison in Oregon, because before I could figure up a good plan to escape, they snatched me off the yard real early one morning and slapped me on a prison transfer bus headed for Leavenworth.

Nowadays they really make a big deal about how I cut my handcuffs off on that bus, make it sound like I'm Houdini or somebody, and they shudder when they read my record, because you just don't cut your handcuffs off unless you're the number one escape artist in the whole world. Those handcuffs used by the U.S. Marshalls are made of hardened steel. They don't cut off.

So let me set the record straight. That was more than a half-century ago. They did things different then. Today, when you are transferred they, the U.S Marshall's Service, bind each prisoner up like a bale of hay. They cuff each prisoner separately, put on the cuffs, attach the cuffs to a belly chain, and last they put on your leg irons, which they also attach to your belly chain. And that's after you get strip-searched and dressed in "sterile" coveralls. You don't take anything with you except a personal property receipt. Your property is shipped separately by mail. Soggy lunches are packed in paper sacks and consist of maybe a slice of lunchmeat, a slice of cheese and maybe an apple, which you eat on the plane or bus while in route and while fully cuffed and chained. If you have to go to the bathroom, well, you figure it out.

In the Alcatraz days, though, U.S. Marshalls were mainly just baby sitters, but today, thanks to new laws which allow them to pursue and arrest fugitives, they are able to fulfill their Marshall Dillon fantasies to the fullest. And they do.

Anyway, in the old days they did things different. When transferring prisoners by bus, they just used one pair of cuffs with a medium long chain for each two prisoners, attaching one cuff to one prisoner and the other to the other prisoner, so that each man had one arm free, no belly chain and no leg shackles. So it wasn't necessary at all to cut the cuff itself, off, I saw that right away. All a guy had to do was cut one tiny link in the soft metal chain that connected one prisoner to his partner and you were free.

Well, we rode all day on that bus bound for Leavenworth and stopped to spend the night in a jail in Ogden, Utah. After we were settled in, the jailer passed out soap and razors and things like that. And, like I said, things were different in those days. Significantly, razors were different. Single-blade razors used single-edged blades, and single-edged blades were big enough and sharp enough to cut through kryptonite. And we wore the same clothes out as we wore in, so it was easy to hide several single-edged razor blades in the belt seam in the top of my pants, and just as easy to cut a link in that raggedy hand-cuff chain.

I paired up with a youngster about my age, and just as crazy, who was more than willing to shorten his sentence, and away we went early that morning on the second leg of our journey to Leavenworth. By the time we reached Little America we had the link in the chain cut all the way through. We took a toothbrush handle and pried the link apart, so all we had to do was simply unhook the separated links and take off. The guards wouldn't notice that the chain was cut as long as we kept the chain stretched tight.

Our plan was to take off in opposite directions when they unloaded us at the jail in Denver. That was our destination for the day. A prisoner who had rode this route before told us we would be unloaded right onto the sidewalk in front of the downtown jail, with pedestrians walking around all over the place, so the guards wouldn't dare fire their guns for fear of hitting somebody. Me, I didn't trust the guards for one second when it came to firing a gun in the middle of a crowd, but guns couldn't shoot around corners, and I was faster than a streak of lightning, so I was all pumped up ready to go.

Great plan, but I guess God had other things to do that day besides watching over idiots, because when we pulled into Denver we didn't go close to downtown, we just kept right on going around and as my heart dropped to the floor we took a turn out in the country and pulled into a brand new jail with a high fence around it and a shot-gun guard standing on top of a building waiting for us. We pulled into a sally-port and then through a second gate and on into the compound. Man, it was just like a small prison and it was so new we could still smell fresh paint as they ushered us inside in pairs of two.

There was nothing we could do, me and my partner, except keep the chain tight so it wouldn't come unhooked, which is what we did. Everything went okay for a little while. Once inside they lined us up in twos, and a guard came down the line unlocking handcuffs, which he threw over his shoulder as he came. When he got to us, he unlocked my cuff, so far so good, then he unlocked my partner's cuff, still okay, the chain held together. But when he went to throw the pair of cuffs over his shoulder one cuff went one way and the other went the other, clanking and bouncing all over the floor. Made one heck of a racket.

Then things came to a complete stop. I tried to look surprised, tried not to laugh, held my breath till I must have turned blue. The guard looked one way, looked the other, looked back, then back again. I wish I could have taken a picture of the expression on his face. Somebody finally figured it out and let loose a snicker. I still tried to be cool but I was about to choke. So was my partner. Finally everybody started laughing so I couldn't hold it any longer. I laughed till tears ran out of my eyes and snot ran out of my nose.

Well, the guards didn't say anything that day, but when we resumed our trip the next day me and my buddy were in leg irons and chains, and when we arrived in Leavenworth we were marched straight to the hole where I remained for about six months until very late one night when they bundled me and three other guys up, and the rest is history.

My buddy wasn't shipped to Alcatraz because I told them it was my idea, which it was.

So there you have it. . But I haven't told you about Oregon yet. That was the roughest one.

*****

CHAPTER TEN

One Saturday morning at Alcatraz I went down to band practice. I went out of guilt, mainly, because I had missed two or three weeks in a row so I figured I'd better show up. Forest Tucker had been giving me some pitiful looks in the mess hall.

Our little band room was in the basement just off the shower room and it was one of the few places in the whole prison where a bunch of guys could go without any supervision by a guard. They just locked us in and took off — I guess they couldn't stand the noise we made, otherwise they would have had somebody watching us.

Forest Tucker was visibly pleased by my presence, as were most everybody else, except maybe the other guitar player; he greeted me politely but didn't seem overjoyed.

Everything started off good. We set up and went through a Duke Ellington arrangement. We went over and over it at least a dozen times, stopping frequently because of its difficulty for some of the horn players. It was hard for me, impossible for the other guitar player who was really getting frustrated. So we gave it a break and played something easy, I forgot what but it was one of those stock arrangements by Benny Goodman or somebody, had a country flavor — one of those songs you can play the chords to just by ear, anticipating when and where to change chords long before it was time to change. I just naturally zipped through it without even thinking, got it right the first time.

Well that did it. At first the other guitar player sat there burning while we played the song again, didn't touch his guitar. And again I played it effortlessly. Then he started talking, not looking at me, just talking in a monotone, said he spent hours every night practicing his guitar, working on songs we were scheduled to work on at the next band practice, and he said I never practiced and just showed up whenever I took a notion and right off the bat played perfectly the songs he had busted his balls all week on and sometimes the week before and the week before that, and I just showed up out of nowhere and played those songs perfectly, he said without slowing down, "You could be a great guitar player you have a gift and you're too lazy to take advantage of it why don't you just stay the fuck away and quit fucking with me."

That's what he said.

Well everybody was surprised, including me. Poor old Forest Tucker almost fainted. But I figured it out quickly because I knew what was wrong with him, the guitar player, and he didn't, and you can't tell a musician with no talent that he has no talent because he truly doesn't know he has no talent, and he can never know. So I just shrugged it off and gave him a good natured smile and said, "Sorry 'bout that, let's play it again, you'll catch on."

Forest Tucker was obviously relieved, for he did not like violence at all, or at least that's what I figured then, and he quickly said let's try it again and he counted it off.

Again I played it perfectly, for it was too easy to mess up, and while I was willing to shrug off the other guitar player's frustration, I was not willing to compromise whatever little talent I had by catering to him musically. That I would not do.

Well, I guess he couldn't stand it anymore, for when the song was over he jumped up, grabbed his guitar by the neck and swung it in a wide arc right at my head. It's a good thing our guitars were hollow-body acoustics and a good thing I threw up my hand or I would have had one hell of a headache. As it was I was able to fend off the guitar enough so that it only gave me a glancing blow before it smashed into the back of my chair with a sound that could only mean the twanging end to that guitar.

Enough. I came out of that chair, handed my guitar to the trumpet player, and tore into that stupid son of a bitch faster than a streak of lightning, tore his raggedy ass up. And a couple of seconds later he was on the floor and I was standing over him with clenched fists. I didn't kick him, because in those days you didn't kick a man when he was down, well usually not, I didn't, unless he was a child molester or a snitch or a — never mind I didn't kick him.

He shook his head, felt his jaw. His nose was bloody, that I could see. I shouted at him, "You stupid son of a bitch! You broke a goddam guitar!" That's all I could think of. We only had two guitars and this dumb son of a bitch broke one all to pieces. Now we only had one.

Well he surprised the hell out of me. He rolled over on his back and made no attempt to get up. He just laid there gazing at me like he'd just made a new discovery. Then he said, "Well at least I found out you really do care about a guitar. You really had me wondering." That's what he said. And that's all he said.

Maybe nobody else knew what he meant, but I did. I said, "Yes I do." And I relaxed and gave him a hand up. Forest Tucker let out a sigh of relief. He had watched the whole thing, probably wringing his hands. At least he hadn't thrown a roll of toilet paper at me.

We took the guy into the shower room and cleaned him up, stuffed some toilet paper up his nose to stop the bleeding. After that we had no more trouble out of him. He was the nicest guy in the world, brought his own guitar, the one he had in his cell, to practice. It was amazing what a good smack in the nose would do for an attitude.

And he was probably right about me being lazy. But I was young and still had forever.

That afternoon I hit the yard. Burgett was walking up and

down with Clyde Johnson, which drew my curiosity because none of our guys hung out with Clyde. He was a good guy though, Johnson was, slight of build, easy going. I didn't know where he worked, but then I remembered him and Burgett had a part-time job on the weekends on the garbage truck which went around the island outside the wall, around the guards' living quarters picking up trash. And then it hit me and I did a double-take. Uh-huh! That was it. And I looked again.

Burgett had been testing his air bags again so time must be getting short. They were walking close together, and every once in a while they stopped and huddled, talking excitedly, stopping whenever anybody walked close to them and then resuming their conversation when they were sure they were alone again. They weren't very cool.

I went on, forcing myself to think about something else just in case a snitch had his radar tuned to my thoughts, which might be exaggerating a bit but not much. You couldn't be too careful.

I wandered behind Jackrabbit hunched over a card table, had a sudden impulse to goose him so I did, goosed him in both ribs. Well, he'd been concentrating real hard and he jumped and gave me an aggravated look, saw it was me and softened up. He said, "When are you going to pump your nuts up enough to play some more bridge." And I said, "Probably never. You're too good for me." And I walked on, but I had a plan. I had borrowed a good bridge book by Charles Goren and I was studying it. My time would come.

I didn't play much softball that summer. Jack Waites and Fat Duncan had gone to the hole again and a couple of other guys had a different routine so the Gullies sort of drifted apart. We didn't have an organized softball league anyway, just a few teams that sort of hung out together. Punchy Bailey still had his team, him and Belew and those guys. They were good. Beat everybody on the yard.

I had known Punchy Bailey up in Oregon in the state joint. I never hung out with him, but I knew him. He worked in the Associate Warden's office as a clerk, but the AW had quit, as had most of the brass, because Warden O'Malley, Beet Face, refused to be tough on the inmates and now the inmates were practically running the place. It was anarchy. They had a ninety percent turnover in guards and staff during my time there. Anyway, the warden was doubling as warden and associate warden, doing both jobs, so Punchy Bailey was clerking for both jobs.

Punchy Bailey had so much power in Oregon that he could assign an inmate to any job in the institution, assign any cell, he could even send you out to the farm, all the way out of the prison if the money was right. And before the big riot, when they got rid of O'Malley and brought in an old gimp-legged warden from the federal prison system, Punchy Bailey had so much power that he was doing the captain's job, making out daily work assignments for the guards, work assignments, vacations and everything else that a captain normally does.

So the first thing the new warden did when he took over was send Punchy Bailey straight to Alcatraz.

At Alcatraz, Punchy Bailey worked in the tailor shop in the cutting room, him and Belew. They cut out the different parts for pants and shirts and things like that from a bunch of stock patterns of different sizes. And they drew new patterns for new clothing items requested by various agencies. The military was the main customer, of course.

Up in Oregon I never talked to Punchy Bailey. We hardheads never talked to politicians. That's what we called anybody who worked for the cops, politicians, which was a dirty word in our limited list of words. But at Alcatraz he, Punchy Bailey, was an okay guy. Everybody talked to him, convicts and cops alike. In fact, whenever the captain and his crew of lieutenants came through the tailor shop, as they did quite often, they passed right by the tailor shop supervisor with just a wave and a brief hello and went straight on into the cutting room, where they usually stayed for maybe an hour talking to Punchy Bailey and Belew, mainly Punchy. They didn't close the door or anything. Punchy wasn't snitching, they just chatted and chatted and chatted, that's how interesting Punchy Bailey was to talk to. He was a genius of conversation, always interesting, always saying just the right thing in just the right way, just natural, none of it put on.

And Belew wasn't far behind him when it came to conversation. Belew was tall and handsome with a fresh schoolboy look and a personality that would disarm the devil.

I don't know why they called Punchy, Punchy. I guess he did look a little like a prize fighter with his thick neck and stocky body. His looks were nothing to brag about. But once he turned those clear eyes on you and started talking you listened. And when it was your turn to talk, he listened with equal interest. His eyes were always clear and guileless and every word he said was the truth on a truckload of bibles.

He was not a con man, I'll say that for him. A con man misrepresents himself as someone he isn't in order to gain something. A con man is deceitful. Punchy was not deceitful, he was just a magnet, a natural leader. People came to him and bestowed him with power and influence as if it were his due. All he had to do was just be himself and everybody else deferred to him. So he was not the "politician" I had thought him to be up in Oregon where I hadn't really known him. He was just Punchy Bailey. And the tide always flowed his way.

Punchy Bailey was a state prisoner, farmed out by the state prison in Oregon to the federal prison at Alcatraz; as such he was eligible for parole in the state of Oregon. The parole board from there came to Alcatraz yearly and held a hearing as required just for Punchy Bailey, but it was just for show because no one could be paroled from Alcatraz, state prisoner or not, and as persuasive as Punchy was he couldn't buck a stone wall. But his argument did make sense, that he should be transferred back to Oregon because state law required a meaningful meeting with the parole board once a year with a meaningful chance to make it. His argument was so clear-eyed logical that the captain at Alcatraz, along with some of the lieutenants and even the warden, old Promising Paul, himself, went to bat for Punchy Bailey so strongly that the warden in Oregon had no choice but to, with great reluctance, accept Punchy back to Oregon.

And once back in Oregon, The Gimp got rid of him real quick, called an emergency meeting of the parole board and paroled him straight to the streets, that's what I heard, and it must have been true because I later learned that he, Punchy Bailey, got a job in Portland as a car salesman and within a short time ran the entire business. Just like old Punchy.

For now, though, Punchy Bailey was still at Alcatraz and had a softball team that beat everybody on the yard. And me, to tell the truth, I didn't like him all that much at all. I'm just trying to be fair and accurate in describing him in case somebody reads this raggedy book. I mean I swore on a stack of bibles and my mother's honor, so I'm sort of beholden to tell the truth whether the truth agrees with my convict code of honor or not.

You may not believe that convicts have such a code, or are even worthy of such a code, but we did just the same, as strong and honorable as any group of people in the world; in fact it was necessary that we have such a code just to live together. For example, stealing from another convict was a serious violation of the code, a violation so serious that it could get you killed. And you didn't piss on a toilet seat without cleaning it up, a violation not as serious as stealing, of course, but one that could get you a bloody nose. And, of course, you'd better pay your debts and you'd better do that on time or give a good explanation why you couldn't.

Whitey Bulger was a convict who lived by such a code. He was just a youngster, himself, maybe twenty-seven or eight, but the streets of South Boston had already toughened him beyond his years. I didn't know him well. We spoke, made a few small bets once in a while, but I knew he always carried himself like a real stand-up convict, always paid his debts and expected as much from everybody he dealt with. He lived by the code. In later years after he got out and made it in the world, he had his old buddy's body exhumed from a pauper's grave, his buddy being Clarence Carnes, "The Choctaw Kid," a full blooded Indian and famous prisoner at Alcatraz who was the only survivor of the deadliest escape attempt in the history of Alcatraz, the "1946 Blastout." Whitey Bulger had his body dug up and he personally transported it in a bronze casket back to the tiny town of Daisy Oklahoma for a proper burial. That's what kind of man Whitey Bulger was, and that's how I remember him—never mind how he got his money; that was business between him and the South Boston mobsters, just business.

One day as we were coming in from work to eat lunch, the water tower started shaking and clanging and the earth started trembling. Scared the shit out of us for a minute, but once we figured out what it was we clapped and cheered wishing the whole island would shake off its foundations and crumble into the bay. No such luck, it was just a little quake and was over quickly; we were locked down and counted and they let us out to eat as usual.

In my cell at night I sometimes walked the floor to burn off a little energy, my legs fueled by testosterone and adrenaline I guess. It was nineteen-fifty-eight and more and more good radio programs were switching to television to be replaced by music and news and talk, so there wasn't much to listen to. I had read all the Zane Grey books at least twice. I studied my borrowed Charles Goren book a lot, preparing for my planned ambush of Jackrabbit on the bridge table. I already had a partner who was really up on Goren.

I noticed on the yard that portly Courtney Taylor was walking and talking with a youngster, the same kid I'd noticed him walking with the past several months. I knew he was schooling the kid on check-cashing but I also suspected Courtney was a little funny, and I don't mean ha ha funny, for he was really bubbling over with it.

Just the week before I had talked to Courtney. He was changing his M.O., he said. He'd bought some U.S. Savings bonds with the money he made in the factory and was studying them with a good possibility that he could counterfeit them. They stored them in a safe in the institution and allowed him to look at them every once in a while. And look he did. He must have had a good memory, for he could talk about them for hours.

The summer dragged on. Every now and then I went up on the bleachers and gazed longingly out to sea, hoping my girlfriend in the red bikini would come back. But she never did.

*****

CHAPTER ELEVEN

It was a clear day in the San Francisco Bay, an unusually clear day. It was so clear that you could maybe see all the way to Hawaii if not for the curvature of the earth. The sky was blue, not a cloud from horizon to horizon. It was broad daylight with the sun in the middle of the sky. There was no smog, no fog, and the wind was calm and the water was calm, and the sea gulls made lazy effortless circles high above. In other words, it was a clear day in the San Francisco Bay.

And a big ship ran smack-dab into the island, into Alcatraz Island. A fleet of ships came in, U.S. Navy ships, wearing their colors proudly, a parade of ships. And as befitting a parade, cannons boomed in salute while sailors dressed in spiffy white graced the decks preparing to invade the city of San Francisco.

And one of their great big ships just moseyed right up smart as you please and ran into Alcatraz Island like that was part of the show or something. Thud, crunch, and that was it. Alcatraz Island grabbed ahold of the bottom of that ship and wouldn't let go. The ship tried to back up, couldn't. Tried to go forward, couldn't. Tried again and again, still couldn't. It was stuck tight.

All the while this was going on us convicts stood on the bleachers hollering and clapping and cheering. A tug of war was going on between that ship and Alcatraz, and we were rooting for Alcatraz. Why, I don't know, but we were.

The cops let us stay up there and watch for a good while, maybe expecting the ship to pull free and be on its way. But when it became obvious that the ship wasn't going anywhere, they ran us in and locked us down. On the way in I took a last look. The island had that ship in a bear hug. Alcatraz was winning.

To this day I still wonder about that ship, how with all its radar and sonar and a thousand human eyes, in broad daylight with the sun shining bright, how a full grown ship of the U.S. Navy could ever run into Alcatraz Island. My lasting memory of it was that it looked like a giant float with four flat tires in the Rose Bowl Parade.

The grounding of the ship was on the news that evening, all over the news. And the radio cop didn't cut it off until the regular time for the radio to go off for the night. The ship was still stuck. From our cells we could hear tugboats chugging all night trying to pull it loose. Finally sometime the next morning they cracked our doors and let us out. And the ship was gone

That's just one of the trivial things that happened at Alcatraz that lazy summer. Another, a whole bunch of garbage washed up on the island shore. And that happened more than once, so much garbage that the sea gulls had a feast, so much garbage that the seagulls grew fat and lazy. They didn't have to hunt for food anymore. All they had to do was just plop down and eat until their bellies got so full they could barely fly. Fortunately, home was only a short distance from the feast. All they had to do was make it to the factory roof and roost until their bellies got empty again.

That winter the garbage was gone. It just stopped washing up as mysteriously as it had begun. And that winter a good portion of the seagull population died. Forest Tucker figured they died from some kind of disease. Burgett figured the guards poisoned them. Me, I didn't say anything but I had a strong suspicion that when they got fat and lazy from all the free food, they no longer had the strength or the will to hunt like they used to, and I wondered if they were like us, or rather if we were like them, that after years in prison where all our needs were taken care of we would lose our will to compete in the free world. It was a scary thought, and one that I didn't share with anyone at the time. But I wondered about it.

I should have been counting my days by then, because I would be getting out next year sometime, free again, less than a year away, except there were two things that kept me from thinking about it too much. First I had lost all my goodtime for my escape attempt on that transfer bus from McNeil Island to Leavenworth. Second, I had a detainer on me from Oregon for escaping from that jail in Portland. So my expectations for getting out anytime soon were vague to say the least. In fact they weren't even on my menu for the near future.

The Oregon detainer was the most serious problem, a big gray cloud on my horizon. I could probably expect to get about five years for escape, and that would mean five years in Oregon State Pen, where I would not be welcome by the guards or staff, especially not by Lieutenant Francis, who hated me with a boiling passion. I remember the day I got out of OSP, having served every day of my four-year sentence. I had already lost all my goodtime, so they couldn't keep me any longer no matter what. Well old Lieutenant Francis hated me so much that he sent a guard down to R&D with instructions to pick a fight with me while I was dressing out, hoping I'd be dumb enough to swing on him and thus fall victim to a new Oregon law which called for a five year sentence for assaulting a guard. This guard called me all kinds of names, but I was too happy to be getting out to take his bait. Lucky for me that another guard was with me who frowned on the whole thing and shushed the guard up enough for me to finish dressing and get out the door. In fact, my dress-out guard escorted me all the way out.

It was a tradition in Oregon for the warden to shake hands

with every prisoner released and wish him the best of luck and all that, but old Gimp wasn't about to shake my hand even if I saved his life. He was nowhere in sight that day, wisely so because I had already vowed not to accept any kind of handshake or anything else from that sorry fucker.

I was eighteen when I went to prison in Oregon. I was sentenced to four years by a judge in Medford who seemed to like the sound of four years, for he gave everybody who came before him the same four year sentence, or so it seemed to me because the same day he sentenced me he sentenced three other guys, all to four years. I got mine because I was sleeping in the back seat of this car parked in front of a house and the cops saw me when I woke up and sat up to stretch my legs, and they thought I was trying to steal the car, I guess, so they arrested me, though how I could steal a car from the back seat, I don't know.

Anyway the judge gave me four years. I'd never been to prison before, but I'd been in reform schools in Kentucky and California, so I wasn't worried about it all that much. That night after the four of us had been sentenced we were told we would be shipping out to prison the very next morning and this news really upset the other three guys. It upset them so much that they couldn't eat their supper that evening. So I volunteered to do them a favor and eat it myself. Which I did. All three of theirs as well as mine. I remember it well because we had beans well-seasoned with pork, which is what I was raised on, beans and pork. I mean Zeb Hackney wasn't about to turn his milk cows into hamburger. He killed a big fat pig once a year and salted it in the sun and then smoked it in the smokehouse, and that's what we ate. And that's what I liked. So I ate well the night before we were shipped off to prison.

When we got there they didn't hold any ceremonies to greet our arrival. They sent us straight to a raggedy old cell house with cells that housed about four people per cell and had a sink but no toilet. They gave us a bucket and told us a guy would come by our cell every morning and pick up the bucket and take it out to Shit Creek and empty it and wash it out and bring it back to us, which he did, a big black convict who would whip your ass in a second if you gave him any shit, uh, any problem.

I got there just when O'Malley became the new warden after a successful riot got rid of the old warden, whoever he was. And I heard the new warden's speech over the earphone radio. He declared that prisoners would no longer be mistreated, would no longer be beaten and starved, that new teachers would be hired so that everybody could get an education, that we would be treated like human beings, and the main thing, that the food in the mess hall would immediately get better.

We cheered the part about the food getting better. I wasn't all that interested in the education part. When I was eighteen I already knew everything. I got dumber as the years went by. Funny how that works.

Anyway, I went wild at OSP. When they cracked the doors in the morning I was gone. They had no controlled movements, no out-of-bounds as long as you didn't climb the high wall that circled the prison, no inside fences, no daytime counts—I think they had a four-o'clock evening count but I don't remember for sure. I know we were out till about nine or ten before we were locked down for the night, and by then I was so tired I went straight to sleep.

I didn't get a job because nobody had to work if he didn't want to, and I didn't want to. Simple arithmetic. But I figured wrong, because one day they snatched me up and put me to work in the mess hall, said they had a rule that all new guys had to take a turn at it if we wanted to eat, so I took my turn. For ninety days, and that was it.

The new warden was good at his word: we were treated okay, more teachers were hired, and the food, well, it wasn't great—it never is when you have a bunch of lazy convicts cooking it—but it was okay.

The new warden meant well, but he had two big problems

to deal with that he hadn't counted on. One, he was too soft-hearted and we ate him alive. Two, many of the high brass from the previous administration, including the superintendent, still worked there, and though they didn't have the power they previously had, they were still in a position to cause problems for the new warden, and they did, every chance they got. O'Malley didn't have the experience to know that he needed to bring in some of his own people to watch his back.

Me, I didn't care one way or the other. I worked ninety days in the mess hall, as required, and quit. There were too many other things to do. Like I quickly fell in with a bunch of guys my own age and we terrorized the cannery, stealing gallon cans of fruit which we sold to the wine makers to make home brew. That was a lot more fun than washing dishes and wiping tables—and we made a little money doing it.

There was Pomeroy and Lewis and Hopper and Gen (the Mexican General, who wasn't a real general but we called him that), and a couple more misfits who took up with us. We hung out a lot in an old vacant building right beside the cannery. The building had no windows and no doors, just big holes where they used to be, and the loading dock of the cannery was right next to it, only about ten feet away, so we could stand in our hangout and watch the action at the cannery and make elaborate plans like drawing up plays for a football game. We had the shoot-out play, which was just a simple run and snatch and run back which any of us could do in the blink of an eye, except for the General, who was good at planning but not all that fleet of foot. Then we had the turn play, where one of us would walk across to the loading dock and ask the guard a question while somebody else did a run and snatch. Then we had the double snatch, where one guy faked a run and snatch and when the guard went after him somebody else would do the real run and snatch. Then we had the sneak play and the relay play, on and on. We made up at least one new play every day. I mean, we were wanted dead or alive by the cannery guards so it was a real tactical challenge.

None of the other prisoners even came close to our hangout, they knew better because our guys could fight if it came down to it and the cannery and vacant building was our territory. Even the guards stayed away, not that they were afraid of us or anything, it's just that while O'Malley was warden the guards more-or-less just secured the perimeter and left us alone. It was anarchy inside the walls.

As an example of how wide open the prison was, one prisoner built a small carnival on the yard, just gathered up the tools and the wood and other supplies from the shops — the carpenter shop and machine shop and plumbing shop and all the small shops along the main prison street — he gathered his materials and built a merry-go-round and a small ferris wheel right out in the yard in front of the domino tables. He built his little private carnival of fun rides to attract the young boys so that he could molest them. That's what he did.

And the guards didn't do a thing about it. They did nothing partly because the new warden didn't order them to do anything about it, and partly, rumor had it, because some of the old brass left over from the old regime told them to do nothing as part of a plot to undermine the authority of the new warden, figuring, I guess, to regain power if the new warden failed to maintain control.

In the early fifties Oregon didn't have any reform school for teenagers. They sent them all to the prison in Salem where they turned them loose on the yard with hardened criminals, murderers, child molesters, crazies, all mixed in together. They had kids as young as fourteen-years old in the Oregon State Prison at that time.

So the carnival man had lots of youthful participants for his free rides.

When it became obvious what he was up to, though, our guys and a bunch of other old convicts took matters into our own hands. We took sledge hammers and crowbars and ball bats, whatever we could pick up, and we hit the yard in the early morning in a misting rain and tore that carnival all to pieces. I mean we made a big trash pile out of it. While we were tearing it down the old carnival guy came out screaming and hollering, which saved us the trouble of hunting him down, so we took that opportunity to solve that problem, too. We tore his ass up.

And that's the last we saw of him.

For the most part, the old convicts looked out for the kids, protected them from the sexual predators and all that, the ones who wanted to be protected, but there were some who preferred to hook up with an older convict for both protection and sex, especially if the older convict had money and power.

The old yard captain, who had a shack right on the corner of the street that went out across Shit Creek to the little yard and the long street that passed the shops on the way to the big yard, the front gate and the cannery, he was a tough old bastard. We called him Cold Slim. The main thing I remember about him was that when he ran up against a convict who was always causing problems, he often gave him some very serious counseling which included: "Why don't you get you a punk and settle down."

That's his exact words, often his recommendation to problem prisoners.

Anyway, besides the underage kids, the prison had its share of full grown sissies, who swished around the yard in cut-off shorts and flowery tops and often got married in a formal ceremony on the little yard up in the boxing ring by a "bonafide" convict preacher with a certificate, vows and all: "Do you take this, uh, sissy to be—etc., etc.."

The reason I'm telling you this is to explain what kind of a prison I was in and set the record straight about how I wound up with thirty-two recorded disciplinary reports and many more incidents that were never recorded. We finally got busted by the cannery cops and I went to the hole for a very long time, a very long time not because of the cannery thing but because I ran into some guys down in the hole who were intent on escaping, which sounded like a great idea to me. These guys, Buck Poe, Al Doolin, Joe Benson, Little Al Brumfield, they were all real genuine all-American convicts. And the shit hit the fan, which is a cliché nowadays but we are the ones who invented it.

The shit hit the fan.

*****

CHAPTER TWELVE

The hole in the Oregon State Penitentiary was in the basement below one of the cell houses. I don't remember the name of the cell house, but I remember every square inch of that hole. Each cell had two bunks, one above the other, and each cell had a sink and toilet with running water, and each cell had a couple of shelves and a fold-out metal desk and that's it, not a lot to remember. I took the top bunk in a cell with Buck Poe, a little old convict with a big mustache and a whole library of stories which he was only too happy to share with me every night after they locked us down. He was a legend.

For one thing he told me all about the big riot that happened just before I arrived at the prison. I had missed it, unfortunately, by a matter of only a few weeks. But I changed the "unfortunately" to fortunately when he told me it was a food strike, not a riot. I'm not fond of food strikes.

But I was wide-eyed with interest as he told me all about it, for Buck Poe was a legend and I was eighteen years old. He said he was the main strategic advisor to the strike leaders, telling them exactly how to win a hunger strike, and win they did, thanks to that advice. First, and most important, he told me, is that if you're going to have a hunger strike or a work strike, any kind of strike, you can't have any violence, can't break windows or destroy any government property or hit a guard or take any hostages, can't do anything to give the cops an excuse to use force, otherwise your strike was doomed to failure. Second, and just as important, you have to keep your fellow prisoners from going to the mess hall to eat, if it's a hunger strike, and that's the hard part. During the food strike at Oregon the leaders had stabbed the first prisoner who tried to go eat, and when the rest of them saw blood that ended that problem.

The inmate population went without food for a full week and won the strike. And they brought in a new warden to right the wrongs at the prison. End of story, except Buck Poe took two hours to tell it, and I listened eagerly to every word, for he was a legend.

In the hole they let us out into the basement corridor every day all day long and locked us back down for the evening meal, and that was the end of our day and it was talking time for Buck Poe.

He really wasn't no joke, though. Every day while we were out for recreation he was sawing on the window bars which he had to do through a thick mesh steel screen using a hacksaw blade attached to a foot-long steel rod he removed from the sink each day. It was tedious work, sawing those bars, but Buck Poe showed great patience doing it. And he quit work early enough each day to conceal the fresh cut in the bar with a gray paste he made out of soap and cigarette ashes. He even had a tiny mirror small enough to fit through the tiny hole in the screen which he could use like a periscope to see behind the cut bar after he applied his paste.

While he was cutting the bars some of us played pinochle, me and Joe Benson and Al Doolin and Jonesy. Little Al Brumfield was in the middle section of the hole, which was separated from our back section by a grill of steel bars, so we couldn't include him in our game. The front section was reserved for death row prisoners.

The noise we made playing pinochle, laughing and

signifying and slamming cards on the floor, helped to cover up the sound of Buck Poe's hacksaw blade. And when we weren't playing pinochle, I passed the time doing other fun things like kicking out light bulbs in the corridor ceiling with our football. We could get just about anything in the hole. All we had to do was holler out the window at somebody we knew and he would get it for us, thus we had a football with which I could kick out light bulbs.

And when we got bored we looked for more exciting things. And like convicts will do we often tested the authority of our prison guards, a probe here a probe there, just to see how far we could go. And if we spotted a weakness we just naturally pushed a little harder to see if we could go even further. And of course a new guard was fair game for some serious pushing.

And the anarchy on the yard began to affect the resolve of the guards in the hole. Old guards quit in ever-increasing numbers. New guards without any experience or training appeared every day, even in the hole. And we found out quickly that we could get away with just about anything.

At first, Doolin and Poe and Benson started running different games on the poor naïve guards, like faking illness in the middle of the night in order to get sleeping pills. They got away with that, got their sleeping pills: yellow jackets, blue heavens, seconals, you name it. The guard would listen to their sad stories, their moans and groans, and go call the hospital and a physician's assistant would come down to the hole and listen to their pitiful complaints, and their sleeping pills would be forthcoming.

Well, when the guards and the PA caught on to what was going on and started ignoring our complaints, we took it up a notch; we started banging on our bars with our metal cups, and hollering and screaming, until we woke everybody up in the cell house above us, and they started hollering and screaming for us to shut up and when we didn't and they were wide awake, we hollered up to them that we had a sick man in the hole, so they just naturally joined in, banging and hollering and screaming until the whole prison woke up and joined in.

And that brought the warden himself down to the hole, Warden O'Malley, and he sent for the PA and told him to give us our pills, whatever it took to shut us up, for by now a good part of the city of Salem was wide awake, the neighborhood nearest the prison anyway, for we made enough racket to wake Rip Van Winkle himself.

After that the guards and PA were quick to tend to our requests.

Me, I wasn't crazy about any kind of pills that would put me to sleep. I slept like a baby without them. But I did my share of hollering and banging when it was necessary, for that was fun enough by itself, never mind the pills.

I think I was still eighteen when I went to the hole for the first time, though I don't remember for sure because I didn't have birthdays.

One day they threw a guy in the hole, threw him in the back section with us. At first Buck Poe was afraid to do any sawing on the bars, afraid the new guy might be a snitch or something, but the guy came out of his shoe with a sock full of white crosses, amphetamine sulfate, and he was all right then, a great guy, our best buddy and all that. I tried a couple of them, just to see what they'd do. Tried a couple more just for good measure. Well, in about thirty minutes my eyeballs popped out of their sockets and my nuts shriveled up to the size of bee bee's and I feared I would have to squat to pee because I had a difficult time finding anything to pee with. Scared the shit out of me at first, but everybody laughed and told me that was normal when you were taking bennies.

And that historic night when they locked us down I out-talked Buck Poe so badly that he finally went to bed and covered up his head, whereupon I took up a conversation with Al Doolin in the cell next door and talked till daylight before I shut up because my throat was raw and my jaw was sore.

Al Doolin was a dangerous man. He was in the hole for stabbing another prisoner. And this wasn't his first time. He told me he'd stabbed a guard a long time ago when he was trying to go over the wall, him and another guy. The guard survived the wound at first, got out of the hospital and did okay for eight or ten months, but then had a relapse from some kind of complications, for it was a stab-wound to the lung and had never fully healed. The guard died. Al got a life sentence for that, would have got the death penalty except that the guard had taken so long to die that the jury couldn't be sure his death was a direct result of the stab wound.

Anyway, we had two Al's in the hole. Al Doolin was a big guy, not fat just big, and Al Brumfield was a little guy. We called Brumfield Little Al, but we didn't call Doolin Big Al, we just called him Al. He had the right to the title, Al, because of the pecking order. You know how that goes.

Little Al got a life sentence for murder. He didn't kill anybody. He was in jail for something else. But he faked an illness of some kind and they took him to an outside hospital where he took off running down the hospital corridor and his escort guard shot and killed a nurse trying to hit him, so they charged Little Al with murder. That's the way it works, the law. It was a busy hospital with doctors and nurses and patients moving up and down the busy corridor and the cop just whipped out his gun and started shooting, shot up the whole hospital, hit the nurse right between the eyes, killed her instantly. The cop, not Little Al. But the law says Little Al killed her because if he hadn't been trying to escape the cop wouldn't have been shooting at him, therefore it was Al's fault. Figure that one out if you can.

Little Al was a quiet guy, had a whole stack of Reader's Digests in his cell, liked to read about nature, you know, birds and trees and things. We were going to let him escape with us, but we didn't expect him to be of much use to us if the going got tough. Buck Poe cut a few bars in the steel grill between our section and the middle section where Little Al celled so he'd be ready to go when the time came.

And he, Buck Poe, cut the deadlock bolt in our doors so we could open our own door with a bent spoon handle any time we wanted, day or night. I don't know how he knew where to cut, for the bolt was completely out of sight and had to be cut through a narrow crack in the door frame just by feel. The good thing, though, is that the guards had no way of telling the bolt was cut. The doors closed normally and locked normally, they just couldn't be deadlocked even though they appeared to be. Buck Poe, I realized was more than just talk. He was a mechanical genius.

And last Buck cut the corner of the window screen where it attached to the window frame so that we could bend the whole corner of the screen up and out to get to the hole where the bars were cut. And all we had to do then was wait for a foggy night. Everything was ready.

And one night when I was sleeping soundly Buck Poe shook me awake and whispered for me to get up and get ready. The fog was in.

I'll have to admit I was scared. This was the real thing and it took a few minutes after being woke up so suddenly for my heart to quit pumping piss. But quit it did, and I crawled out of bed and got dressed. Everybody had to carry something, some homemade rope to tie a chicken ladder together, some tools, knives and things. Count time was nearing, so we waited for that, got back in bed with our clothes on and waited.

The guards came through counting, shining their flashlights. We laid quietly until they left and went over to the other side, then we popped our doors open with our bent spoon handles. It was time to roll. Buck Poe and Al Doolin went out first. There was a big square wall fan over beside the window which hid them from view of the guard up front in case he came back to our side. They pried the corner of the window screen up and popped the bars out one by one. Buck Poe had left just a little sliver of each bar uncut so they'd stay in place, but they popped loose easily. He motioned for the next two to come out, me and Joe Benson, so we did, hid behind the fan. Then the next two, Jonesy and Little Al. They hadn't bothered to wake up Little Al, figuring to leave him behind if he wasn't ready on his own, but here he came, Little Al, popped the bar out of the grill and scampered behind the fan. He had seen the fog and been ready. So there we were, six of us hiding behind that big fan. Everything was good so far.

But Joe Benson had forgotten something he was supposed to bring with him, so he went back to his cell to get it and that's when the guard, who must have forgotten something himself, spotted him cutting across the corridor. At first, we weren't sure whether the guard had actually seen him, for the guard stopped and looked for just a few seconds and then disappeared, so we kept going just as planned. Buck Poe went out the window first, then Al Doolin right behind. They began crawling along the bare ground toward some high bushes that would give them cover. Me and Joe Benson were next.

At that moment, though, we spotted two guards with flashlights coming down the side of the building heading right for Poe and Doolin, who were still on the ground, crawling. The guards spotted them and moved up quickly to head them off, shined their flashlights in their faces and hollering at them to get up off that ground and surrender.

Well, at that point I figured it was over, that Poe and Doolin would be marched back to the hole and locked down and we might as well go back to bed. And I was ready to do just that. I mean, what else could we do. We were busted cold turkey. Finished.

Except Buck Poe and Al Doolin didn't figure it that way. They came up off the ground, all right, but not to surrender. Instead they got right up in the guards' faces and did some serious hollering of their own, then they relieved the suddenly willing guards of their flashlights, their caps, which they put on their own heads, and their badges. I saw all this with my own surprised eyes. Man, Poe and Doolin weren't nobody to mess with, and those guards realized it real quick.

Me, I caught on real quick, too, and I squeezed my skinny ass through those bars and joined the party. When everybody was out, we escorted our captives down the foggy path to the construction area where they were building a new segregation building (our future home, I guessed). They had a bunch of lumber there, two by fours and such, and once we got there everybody started doing their jobs while the captured guards stood by and watched. We picked out the longest two by fours and a bunch of short sawed-off ends and began building our chicken ladder.

We spotted two more flashlights coming through the fog and Al Doolin, busy with the ladder, said, "Somebody go up and capture those guards." So, all pumped up by then, I said, "I'll go," and away I went. Somebody came with me but I don't remember who, for by then I was convinced that I could capture a whole army of prison guards single-handed. By the time they got the ladder built another two guards came down the path, so a couple of guys went and intercepted them. So then we had six captured guards, and since there were six of us, everything worked out just right, for we had a guard's cap for each of us.

Ladder built, it was time to go. Surprisingly it was Little Al Brumfield who led the way. And there was nothing wimpy about his purposeful stride. He headed straight for that back wall, jaw set, back straight. And he didn't stop till we got there, us and the six hostages coming up behind. Another setback, by then they had guards posted along the catwalk on the wall between the guard-towers. We couldn't see them clearly, they were just gray foggy shadows, but we saw their flashlights and they saw ours. They hollered at us, must have seen our caps and mistook us for guards for they questioned us about what was going on. So we answered back, said we were looking for escaping prisoners who broke out of the hole, and we asked them if they'd seen anything. When they said no, we told them we were going to split up and scour the compound till we found them, and we retreated into the fog until we were out of sight. We stopped to talk it over, not sure what to do now. We certainly couldn't hit the wall with all those guards up there. They had guns for sure and would recognize us before we got to the top.

It was then that Little Al Brumfield once again took the lead. "Let's go get the box car," he said calmly but firmly. And we followed him, still escorting our captured guards. Plan B.

The box car was parked on its track beside the laundry. The tracks led downhill, across the railroad bridge which crossed Shit Creek, and then to the back gate and thus out of the prison. But the derail was thrown and locked to its post with a padlock. No problem, Little Al took a guard with him and headed down the hill. When he neared the derail he was well within sight of a guard tower even through the fog, But Little Al paid no attention to that. He snapped that lock hasp with one hard jerk of the hardened steel sink plunger, switched the derail back to the main track and was back with us in no time at all.

Well, we asked our captured guards to help us push the boxcar, which they did. We pushed it about halfway down the hill and when it was rolling good we jumped on. The guards, left standing, decided they'd had enough, I guess, for the last I saw of them they were running for the control room. Man they could run.

Downhill we went, gathering speed quickly. I was clinging to a ladder on the side of the boxcar, on the side away from the gate tower so he couldn't get a shot at me. Some guys were inside the car, others rode on the back. The car sped across the railroad bridge. I hung on tight. The gate was coming up fast. It was a big solid metal gate. The boxcar hit it with a loud crunch, nearly throwing me loose from my perch. I heard gun shots, more gun shots. The boxcar slowed on impact, but it was going through, going through, still going through — slowing, slowing.

It stopped dead still. It sprung the gate out far enough for us to get through. I saw freedom. I jumped down and headed that way. But then suddenly the steel gate, stretched to its limit, sprung back in pushing the boxcar with it with such force that the boxcar rolled back halfway to the bridge. And freedom was gone. The gate was back in place. I heard more gunfire. Looked up and saw the guards through the fog. They had simply left the tower and walked down the catwalk atop the wall and were directly above us busting caps like crazy.

How they kept from killing us all I don't know, the excitement I guess. I mean bullets were flying all over the place and everybody was scrambling this way and that. Finally, everybody, including me, ran for the stopped boxcar, then to the bridge. We took cover on some rocks underneath the bridge.

The guards kept firing round after round in our direction, shot up the boxcar, shot the hell out of Shit Creek, kept shooting till they either ran out of bullets or got tired of shooting. The night was finally quiet.

We were pinned down and there was nothing else we could do. So we smoked some cigarettes and talked. We knew the cops wouldn't be coming for us until daylight for they wouldn't want any part of us in the fog and darkness.

We had failed. But not really, for we had made a good try at it, and I had learned a lot about everybody including myself. I had done my part. And I had especially learned a lot about Little Al Brumfield and about bravery.

*****

CHAPTER THIRTEEN

When the sun came up and the fog lifted they came after us. They came with guns, they came with a whole arsenal of guns: tommy guns, shot guns, rifles, pistols, they came with everything they had. Led by Warden O'Malley, himself, they came to get us out from under that bridge one way or the other. O'Malley had repeatedly restrained his guards from using physical force, including guns, on us for anything that happened inside the prison short of murder, but he showed no such restraint now, for he drew the line on prisoners going over his wall, or under it or through it.

O'Malley looked haggard, like he'd been up all night. He also looked angry and his face was red as a beet. So we, uh, came out from under that bridge with our hands up as ordered. We were not suicidal.

They marched us back to the hole, put us back in our cells, our same cells, except our mattresses were gone. They gave us one wool blanket, a towel and a roll of toilet paper, and that's about it. They explained with a smile that they had to tear our mattresses up looking for hacksaw blades. They didn't bother to explain that they weren't in any hurry to bring new ones, but we caught on after a few nights of sleeping on those hard steel bunks.

They welded all the bars back in place. They checked our

doors, couldn't see anything wrong with them, so they fired the guard who was working the hole on the night we escaped on the grounds that he, himself, must have unlocked the doors and let us out.

That first day back in our cells I noticed some blood on my pants, and on inspecting my left leg noticed that I had been slightly wounded, nothing serious but it was seeping blood so I told a guard and they took me to the hospital. An X-ray showed that I just had a bullet fragment lodged shallowly in my upper leg. The doctor squirted some freezing stuff on the wound and cut out the fragment, no problem, then bandaged it up.

While this was going on the convict attendants and nurses watched me in awe, like I was Jesse James or somebody. The newspapers and radio news programs labeled us "The Halloween Six" because our escape attempt happened to occur on Halloween night because that's when the fog rolled in. I guess Mama Nature decided to spice up her Halloween party a bit with a wild escape to go along with her witches and goblins and things. She could have been more attentive to that stubborn railroad gate.

They eventually gave us back our mattresses and some of our personal property, pictures and letters and such. I had no pictures or letters but I was glad to get back my box of junk which included my football; I hadn't expected to get that back, the football. And when they finally let us out of our cells again for recreation I resumed my passion for kicking out light bulbs.

Warden O'Malley still refused to let the guards come down on us hard like they wanted to do, and at eighteen-years old and having never been in a real prison I figured the way we got away with everything was normal behavior in all prisons, despite stories by Buck Poe and Al Doolin of how the old superintendent and his goon squad used to bust heads and take names before the big strike. And we took up where we'd left off banging on the bars with our tin cups and raising general hell when we got bored. Once we piled a bunch of junk, including an old mattress, out in the middle of the corridor and set it on fire and almost killed ourselves and everybody else. And once we got hungry and captured a couple of guards and demanded that the kitchen cook us some eggs and bacon and biscuits and gravy. And they did.

During the bacon and egg standoff, before they agreed to our demands, Lieutenant Francis appeared at the top of the stairs with a machine gun. He wanted to start shooting, but the warden waved him off and talked to us directly.

We won that confrontation, but we didn't win them all. Lieutenant Francis had survived the transfer of power from the old regime to the new and he didn't like the new at all. According to talk he had been a terror in the old days, supervising the physically crippling beatings of prisoners, ordering the practice of striping a prisoner naked in the old hole in the middle of winter with windows opened wide to let the winter wind drop the temperature to near freezing, which meant the naked prisoner had to stay on his feet and keep walking or freeze to death.

So, remembering the good old days, Lieutenant Francis seized on every opportunity that came his way to remind us of how things used to be. Him and Cold Slim, the old yard captain and another survivor of the old regime, were pretty much of the same mind when it came to control and discipline, except Cold Slim was a professional prison guard who didn't take confrontation personally to the point of a consuming desire for revenge like Lieutenant Francis did. The yard captain always carried himself with dignity and he would bust your head if it came down to it, but he didn't go looking for somebody's head to bust, while Lieutenant Francis looked for any such opportunity.

He, Lieutenant Francis, was on duty one night when we were raising hell down in the hole. And it just so happened that the warden was away on vacation and his associate wardens had quit, so Cold Slim was in charge of the Oregon

State Penitentiary. So here they came, the captain and Lieutenant Francis and about a half-dozen guards they must have hand-picked for I didn't recognize any of them, here they came wide open and ready with clubs and tear gas guns and real attitudes.

I was standing up close to my door minding my own business banging on the bars for some reason, I don't remember why exactly, but I was banging on the bars minding my own business when Lieutenant Francis, himself, appeared in front of my door, and before I could say hello he raised a teargas gun and shot me right in the chest and knocked me stumbling backwards all the way to the back of my cell where I sat down with a plop right on the commode. I was stunned, unable to speak for a good minute. The breath was knocked clean out of me. And I couldn't see because I had tears in my eyes.

In addition to being physically stunned by the blow of the tear gas bomb or grenade or whatever it was, I was surprised that a prison guard would do that to me when I had previously been invincible. That was me, invincible, bullet proof, the baddest eighteen-year old kid in the State of Oregon, badder than Billy the Kid by a country mile, and here I was sitting on my ass on the toilet stool with the breath knocked out of me and worst of all, I was crying.

Finally, when I got over the shock, I jumped to my feet cussing, ran to the front of my cell in a sea of tears and grabbed the bars still cussing. Lieutenant Francis was no longer in front of my cell. I heard other bangs and more cussing down the line, so I guess they were popping everybody. And pop everybody they did, whether they were raising hell or not, and then they left just as suddenly as they'd come.

Buck Poe, my cellie, had been reading a book when it all happened, but he was no longer reading because he was crying like me and cussing too, but he had sense enough to grab a towel and wet it in the sink and smack me in the face with it. "Breath through that," he hollered and then covered his own face with a wet towel.

Well, with everybody choking and crying and cussing there wasn't anything left to do except raise some more hell, only louder this time because everybody in the hole was pissed off by now. We rocked the building.

Which did no good. Lieutenant Francis and his gang ignored us, hoping we'd drown in our own tears, I guess, but when we didn't here he came back, him and his whole goon squad. The gas had cleared out enough to see by then. He stopped in front of my cell again. This time he ordered the cell opened and when it was he stepped back and a big burly guard grabbed me by the front of my shirt and snatched my skinny ass out of that cell and slung me up against the corridor wall like I was nothing. And then they started whacking me with bully sticks and when I went down they kicked me and whacked me some more, and when Buck Poe started out of the cell to help me out they smacked him so hard he landed in a broken heap in the back of the cell.

That really pissed me off, when they hit Buck Poe like that, for he was just a little old man who couldn't have done much damage in the first place. When I was eighteen I was made out of rubber, so their blows hadn't really hurt me that bad. I came up off that floor swinging. I mean I fought like crazy. I got in one good blow to Lieutenant Francis, smacked him right in his big nose and heard him yelp with pain, but then I was on the floor again. This time they beat me and kicked me till I was dead, or at least I thought I was dead. They beat me until I couldn't move any more. And then they beat me until I lost consciousness.

I woke up the next day sore all over. Somebody had put me in bed, which is where I stayed most of the time for the next few days. Buck Poe fared no better. That one big blow that had sent him flying, had hurt his tail bone when he landed and he had to sit on a small rubber inner tube for a long time after that.

Me, I healed quickly and was up banging on bars again within a couple of weeks. I had taken my first ass-whipping and had my first taste of what a real prison was like. And I didn't complain about it, for as stupid as I was I was still smart enough to realize I may have had it coming. So call it even.

But Lieutenant Francis didn't see it that way. There was no such thing as even with him. He dogged me every chance he got for the rest of the time I was there.

They kept no record of that incident, of course; they only keep records of what you do to them, not what they do to you, thus no incident report was written.

Why were we banging on the bars and raising hell to begin with when all we had to do was behave like decent law-abiding convicts and they wouldn't be dogging us at all? What? Are you kidding? Do I really have to explain that? We were in prison. We were in the hole in prison. Imagine yourself locked in your bathroom. Imagine your bathtub replaced with a double bunk so that now all you have is a sink, a toilet and a bunk and a door that won't open, that won't ever open except when they let you out into your living room once in a while for exercise but you can't go outside, you can't ever go outside where the sun is shining, you can see it out the window but you can't go there, you can't go there for days and weeks and months, maybe you can never go there for when they lock you in your bathroom they don't tell you how long you're going to be there, you're just there, period. I'll guarantee you'd be banging on the bars, probably with your head. At least we had sense enough to use tin cups to bang with.

Now imagine they throw Buck Poe in the bathroom with you to tell you stories and I'll guarantee you'll commit suicide long before he quits talking.

Stories get old. In the hole in the Oregon State Prison I was getting tired of Buck Poe's stories, legendary or not. I liked him a lot and he liked me, but we began to notice little picky things about each other that were irritating. Like he liked to take naps, but I was young and full of energy and had not yet learned to take naps. And he snored in his sleep. And he often forgot to wipe the toilet bowl rim clean after he took a piss. On and on, little things that I'd begun to notice.

I'd once heard it said that a man wouldn't be able to survive six months in a cell with his own wife without one of them killing the other and that after a judge heard the story he'd have no choice but to rule it justifiable homicide, no matter who killed who. And that was pretty much the truth, I guess. A few days was all right, even a few weeks. After that it was cruel and unusual punishment.

In fact in later years, when the U.S. Justice Department took over temporary management of some state prisons that were found guilty of unspeakably bad conditions in their treatment of prisoners, it was ruled that small, two-man cells were, indeed, cruel and unusual punishment, and guidelines were set for the exact minimum space in square feet that each prisoner was entitled to in a locked cell. This became the Law of the Land for a number of years and worked out real well. But then, as prisons became more and more crowded, prison administrators presented a suit in federal court to overturn those guidelines, and they won. A federal judge in Cincinnati, Ohio said words to the effect that since prisoners were let out of their cells for recreation during the daytime hours, the square feet of the day room and all common areas were to be counted when figuring the space a prisoner was entitled to. Therefore, a two man cell, no matter how small, was not cruel and unusual punishment.

His ruling still stands today and allows massive overcrowding in every prison and jail in the United States of America. Way to go, judge.

Anyway, I guess Buck Poe was getting tired of my ways too, because one day he packed up his few belongings, including his little rubber donut for his sore tailbone, and moved to another cell, no hard feelings, and left me with a single cell all to myself. Which suited me just fine, for now I had the perfect cell partner: me. And for a while that worked out just fine. Now that I was alone I was able to expand to fill my whole cell, whereas my personal space had previously been confined to my nest up in the top bunk. Now I was bouncing off walls. But even that got tiresome. After a few months of solitary confinement I couldn't even stand my own company and I had to get out of that cell every day when they opened the doors for recreation just to get away from myself. True story.

One day they threw a guy in the hole, threw him in the cell with me. His name was Bob Something, I don't remember his last name. He was a short guy, but what he lacked in height he made up for in width, and his width provided a good canvas for tattoos for he was covered with them, his upper body anyway. He said he was in prison for dealing dope, heroin mainly, and that he'd been busted coming up Highway 99 from L.A. on his bike, busted in Southern Oregon somewhere.

Well I looked at him in awe and asked him how in the world he could pedal a bicycle all the way from L.A. hundreds of miles to Oregon, and he tilted his head back and surveyed me like he was trying to figure out if I was making fun of him or something, and when he saw I was serious he said no, no, a *bike, a hog,* not a bicycle, a Harley. I guess that was his first inkling of how dumb I was, but I figured out pretty quickly that he was talking about a motorcycle not a four-footed hog so I didn't make that mistake. He was a biker. Ah hah!

We didn't have many bikers in the Oregon prison, and we didn't have many dope peddlers, a few heroin dealers but that's about it. And I listened with youthful interest as he told me about dealing dope. He said heroin was where the money was. He didn't fool with anything else because there wasn't any money in anything else. Benzedrine, white crosses, were semi-legal and you could get a whole fruit jar full of them at a truck stop for practically nothing, so there was no money there. And you could buy benzedrine and wyamine inhalers across the counter at any drug store, so there was no money there, and methamphetamine, which had been around since the thirties and sold as desoxephedrine or methedrine, no money there either. And cocaine, that was just a recreational drug for rich people and there wasn't much demand for it. And marijuana, that was too bulky to haul all the way from L.A. on a Harley, so Bob Something just dealt in heroin where the money was.

I was impressed with my new cellie, a genuine biker and dope dealer.

He also told me the reason he got thrown in the hole was that they busted him with a bag of heroin in his locker, said somebody must have snitched on him because a guard came straight in his cell and went straight to his locker, so he must have already known it was there, but then he scoffed and said they didn't get his main stash, though, where he kept his money and most of his dope.

When he said that a warning bell went off in my head, for it didn't make sense that a real dope dealer would tell a complete stranger about his stash like that. But I didn't say anything.

He went on to tell me he was saving his money to buy a transfer to the farm, outside the wall. He said a convict clerk named Punchy Bailey, who worked in the warden's office, was halfway running the prison, behind the scenes, of course, but he handled every cell move, every work transfer, you name it, he had more power than the guards themselves. In fact if a guard wanted something done, he often didn't bother going to the warden, he went to Punchy Bailey. Faster and easier that way.

Well he, Bob the Biker, said Punchy Bailey could get him a ticket to the farm for five-hundred dollars, and he, Bob the Biker had over five-hundred dollars in real green money in his stash, so ten days from now when he got out of the hole he was changing his address to a plush rural farm outside these prison walls. That's what he said.

Strike two. Something wasn't right with this guy.

Strike three wasn't long in coming. He said he had a bottom bunk pass, and he showed it to me with just a little too much smugness on his face. I looked at it, and sure enough it was a real bottom bunk pass, all right, signed by the old quack doctor and the captain. Some people with medical issues that prevented them from climbing up to a top bunk had them. I figured anybody who could wrestle a motorcycle all the way to California and back ought to be able to climb to a top bunk, but I didn't argue with him, he had a legitimate pass. But I also figured the only "hog" he ever rode was the four-legged kind, and that he was a phony.

But he only had ten days, so I let it go. I moved my mattress to the top bunk and climbed up into my nest, retracting my soul to fit my new nest-sized boundaries.

Guys they usually threw in the hole were sentenced to a definite number of days of hole time, while guys like me and Poe and Doolin were segregation prisoners with indefinite sentences, which meant forever for all we knew, which was getting a little tiresome and which we were planning to change in the near future as soon as we figured out how.

Bob Something slept all day and was up all night, one of those kind of people, which was okay but that made it hard to get any private bathroom time because when I had to go during the daytime when we were out for rec I didn't want to wake him up and ask him to leave the cell and I didn't want to go at night with him there. I mean it was just a matter of respect, you for him and he for you, but he had no such respect, so one day when I was out for rec and he was snoring away, I asked Buck Poe, who was playing cards with Al Doolin and Joe Benson and the guys, if I could use the bathroom in his cell, and of course he said yes. Like I said, I didn't want to wake my cell partner up. Out of respect you never wake a sleeping convict. Golden rule.

But Al Doolin, who I guess had for days been watching that problem develop, didn't live by any such rules when the situation called for action otherwise. He laid his cards down, walked over and picked up an empty tin cup, opened the door to my cell, which, like I said, I had closed out of respect for my cellie, Al Doolin opened that cell door and banged like hell on the steel bars nearest my sleeping cellie's head. "Wake up, the world's on fire!" Al Doolin shouted.

Bob Something raised his head with a jerk, but I guess he didn't comprehend what was going on, for his head plopped back down and he resumed snoring instantly.

Al Doolin had an answer for that. He grabbed my cellie's blanket, pulled it all the way off of him with a violent jerk and slung it across the corridor. "Get up and get out of that cell, asshole!" he shouted, but he didn't wait for a response, he grabbed ahold of a sleeping arm with both hands and pulled the arm, with a big tattooed body attached to it, out of bed and all the way out of the cell and halfway across the corridor. That got my cellie's attention. He was awake now. But Al Doolin wasn't finished. He kicked him twice for good measure, kicked him hard right in the butt. Now my cellie was really awake. He scrambled on hands and knees and came to a sitting rest with his back against the corridor wall and a wild-eyed look on his face, but I guess he didn't like what he saw in Al Doolin's eyes, for he made no effort to get up.

Al Doolin then addressed him in plain convict language, told him that he, my cellie, was to get up out of bed every morning when everybody else did and get out of the cell so that people, me, could have some privacy to wash up or shave or jack off or take a "goddam shit," whatever! And he left no doubt that he meant it because he punctuated the "whatever" with a final wild kick that was received with a yelp from Bob, the ex-biker, who scrambled to a corner in the back of the corridor and sat in that corner the rest of the day with very little movement.

I grinned at Al, shaking my head in wonder, and he grinned back then sat down and resumed playing cards as if nothing had happened. And that was the end of that. My cell partner was a model prisoner for his final days in the hole.

And when he left I moved my mattress back to the bottom bunk. I had a single cell again, just me and myself, and I got along with myself just fine from that day on.

And, yes, Judge Something from Cincinnati, a two-man cell is cruel and unusual punishment.

*****

CHAPTER FOURTEEN

We figured if we were going to get our hole sentences changed from indefinite we were going to have to do something pretty spectacular, because they weren't about to do it out of the goodness of their hearts. We had tried sending in written requests to the warden, and we had tried filing a suit in state court in Salem. We really hadn't expected either of those plans to work, and they hadn't. So —

So we did what we should have done to begin with. We rioted.

They had never discovered how we had opened our cell doors when we escaped. We could still come out of our cells any time we wanted. But we had kept quiet about it all this time, and now it was time for surprise, surprise! However we had to fix a couple more doors because guys had moved around and changed cells here and there, so Buck Poe fished a couple of hacksaw blades out of his stash and we went to work cutting dead bolts in the extra doors. But this time they may have heard us cutting, because one day Lieutenant Francis came in with some guards when we were locked down for count and they started snooping around tugging on the window screens and opening and closing doors, checking to see if they locked properly.

We thought they were satisfied when they left without

finding anything, but when they failed to reopen our doors we knew something was wrong. And sure enough here they came back shortly and they came with hammers and started methodically banging on our cell bars. That was the standard method of detecting sawed or partially sawed bars. They just listened to the ringing sound of each bar as they struck it with a hammer or mallet and if they struck a bar that had been cut a different sound came from that bar, a different pitch altogether. Well those guards pounded every one of our cell bars and then they pounded the grill bars between the sections, while Lieutenant Frances paced up and down snooping here and there. Once he stopped in front of my cell and looked at me for a while. I didn't know what he was thinking but I knew it was nothing good. Finally he went on.

When all our bars checked out okay, they all left, but they reappeared outside the building and pounded all the window bars. That done they disappeared again and a long time later the regular guard opened our doors and let us back out of our cells. Figuring they might come back to shake down, Buck Poe stashed our blades and we didn't do any sawing for a couple of days.

What was scary was we didn't know how they'd heard the relatively quiet sound of the hacksaw blade what with all the noise we were making while Poe was working, and we talked about it in whispers for fear the walls had ears. We waited the entire weekend before we resumed our cutting. This time we posted lookouts and made even more noise to cover the sound. But we'd barely got started when a crew of guards led by Lieutenant Francis rode in on us at full speed. They appeared suddenly and rushed down the corridor, slinging open the grill doors and leaving them open.

I happened to be in my cell getting a fresh pencil to keep score with when they reached the back section, and when Lieutenant Francis saw me that's where they stopped. He, Lieutenant Francis, ordered me out of my cell and up against the wall where they shook me down good and then went in my cell and commenced to tear it apart. The Lieutenant stayed outside to watch me. He also watched everybody else and wouldn't let anybody move. Everybody was just sort of frozen where they were.

Buck Poe had been working in a cell near the back and had managed to get the hacksaw blade out of sight when they rushed in, but I knew he hadn't had time to put it in his stash and conceal it right and if they shook him down they'd find it for sure. It was fortunate that the Lieutenant had such a dislike for me that he shook me down first, otherwise they'd probably have seen Buck Poe where he was and busted him cold turkey.

But, with everybody frozen in place they'd get to him next. Lieutenant Francis was already eyeing him. There wasn't much we could do except—except maybe create a distraction.

When the opportunity presented itself I had no choice but to take it. A guard came out of my cell with a football. My football. He showed it to Lieutenant Francis like he'd made one heck of a score, he'd found a football, of all things. He handed it to Lieutenant Francis who took it in the palm of his hand and gave it a perplexed look.

Me, I remember that moment well, what I said and did, what they said and did, I remember every word and every action. What I said was, "Hey, that's my football."

Well, they looked at me, and Lieutenant Francis sort of tossed the ball up a couple of times in the palm of his hand and said, "It's mine now."

And me, I suddenly lunged and grabbed that football out of the palm of his hand and ran like hell. Through the grill gate I went, through the middle section, through the next gate, all the gates having been left open in their mad dash to catch us red-handed. I sped past the death row cells really flying and skidded to a stop when I came to the locked grill that separated the hole from the guards' area. I turned and laughed like hell and I tossed that football way up toward the ceiling, twirling it mockingly.

That's all it took, they came after me on the run, keys jangling, faces red. I backed up against the bars and bent over like I was a running back ready to take the hike from center and when they got about half way through death row, I took off straight for them. If there was one thing I could do it was run. I cut right and then left and I dodged this way and that, and even though they grabbed at me I broke loose and was off again, the ten, the fifteen, the twenty the fifty the forty the thirty the twenty the ten the five, TOUCHDOWN! I even spiked the ball and did a little dance to emphasize my brilliant touchdown run.

They came puffing up behind me out of breath and mad as hell. I saw that Buck Poe was out at the card table. He gave me the okay sign so I knew he'd successfully stashed everything, so I surrendered with a big grin. I was pretty proud of my touchdown dance, but it was nothing compared to the dance old Lieutenant Francis and his boys put on my skinny ass, but they waited until they got everybody locked down and shook down. When they didn't find anything they came after me.

When they got through with me I hurt like hell for a few days, but like I said, when I was eighteen I was made out of rubber so even though each kick was enough to bend me out of shape I sort of popped back to my original form like a Rubbermaid garbage can and within a couple of days I was on my feet again. I had taken a pretty good professional ass-whipping, professional because they didn't kick me in the face or head, only in the body where the scuffs and bruises wouldn't show in case the warden or somebody came through.

The warden must have got wind of it, though, because the next day he came down to the hole with the prison doctor in tow and they cracked the door and looked me over good, made me take off my shirt and then my pants. The doc examined my bruises, asked me how I got them and I answered that I'd slipped on a bar of soap in the shower — standard answer. I mean as much as I disliked Lieutenant

Francis I still figured it was wrong to snitch on him. I'd once heard a good convict say if you'd snitch on a guard you'd likely snitch on a convict too if they squeezed your nuts a little. And, anyway, snitching on a guard was a little too much like whining. I knew when I grabbed that football from old Lieutenant Francis and took off down the corridor for my heroic touchdown run that I was subject to a pay-back of some kind, considering who I was dealing with, so I didn't feel it was right to whine about it. Not everybody shared this view, but, well, I had to look at myself in the mirror every day, not them. I didn't snitch on him. Nor did the warden expect me to. He was soft on the treatment of prisoners, but he was no fool.

I had no bones broken, no permanent damage that the doctor could see, so he gave me some aspirin and told me to walk slow, and then they left.

Warden O'Malley transferred Lieutenant Francis to another post where he no longer came in contact with us, and he assigned the guards who had been in on the ass-whipping to tower duty, which was considered by most guards to be the worst job in the world, sort of like solitary confinement. How did we know all this? The convict grapevine, while not always accurate, was nevertheless faster than the speed of sound. We often got the word, even in the hole, before the guards did. I once heard a guard, when asked a question by another guard, say I don't know, go ask a convict, they know before we do.

Anyway, we didn't see Lieutenant Francis again for a long time, but we were cautious about resuming our sawing because we were convinced somebody, maybe a snitch in the cell house directly above the hole, was listening for it. So we decided to cool it for a while.

The days drug on. I'd lost my football, so I couldn't kick out light bulbs anymore, but that was all right because I was tiring of the whole thing anyway. Time was wearing us out, even me. I got my days and nights mixed up for a while, as did everybody else. We started sleeping all day and talking and smoking cigarettes and drinking coffee all night. They, the prison, furnished us with sacks of Bull Durham tobacco, and we saved our cup of coffee from breakfast and heated it up at night with a toilet paper "bomb." Me, I didn't talk all that much, but I did a lot of walking back and forth in my cell.

We finally got our days and nights straightened out, but we knew we had to do something pretty soon. We were bored shitless, simple as that. Time was wearing us out, our indefinite hole sentences, not knowing when or if we would ever get out. At eighteen I was way too young for that shit.

Eighteen? Well, maybe nineteen or twenty, I didn't have birthdays. In prison a birthday is just another day. Christmas was okay—that's when Santa Claus brought the Christmas bags and we got a good Christmas dinner, so we kept track of Christmas, all right, so, let's see, I'd been in prison for two Christmases, in the hole for one, so, man, I'd been in the hole a long time—with no end in sight.

No more fun and games. We decided to go with what we had and not take a chance on doing any more cutting. We had enough doors fixed to give us a good start, anyway. The prisoners out first could get the key and let everybody else out. So late one night we started banging on the bars to get their attention, and when the hole guard, along with two more guards, came down to check on us, we popped our doors and captured them. Surprise! No problem, they were new guards and easy to capture. And, as planned, we unlocked all the doors in all three sections, including the death row cells.

Then we went over to the other side and opened all the cells over there. There was another side to the hole, which I'd never seen, but it was about the same as the side I was on and had about the same number of prisoners. Now, everybody was out, wild eyed awake and ready to roll. We told them what the deal was, and, of course, they were all for it.

The guards were white with fear. We tried to assure them that we would let no harm come to them, and that seemed to calm them down a little, but I don't think they were entirely convinced, and in the end we assigned a couple of burly convicts to guard the guards to make sure nobody messed with them. And Al Doolin, himself, made a little speech, just a few simple words, actually. "Don't fuck with these guards," and that ended any contrary speculation in anybody's mind, for everybody in the prison knew Al Doolin could back up what he said. As a result the guards were treated that night as if they were members of an endangered species. And the mob, with nobody to beat up, went looking for child molesters.

The two death row prisoners hadn't come out of their cells. They had closed their doors and now huddled in fear in the back of their cells. We really didn't know much about them, the death row guys. They never came out of their cells, all they did that we could see was crochet doilies and things and wait quietly to die, and the preacher came down to the hole once in a while to tend to their souls, so we figured they were some kind of baby-rapers or something, because baby-rapers and child molesters and such always carry a heavy load of guilt which they usually try to unload on Jesus Christ or whatever god will listen to them.

There were so many child molesters in the Oregon prison that it would have been impossible to rid the world of all of them, so we usually more or less left them alone as long as they kept quiet and stayed out of sight. We dealt with molesters like the carnival guy, who, like I said, built some carnival rides on the yard to attract the kids so he could molest them, we dealt with him real good. And there was another molester, an old rawboned braggart with a scraggly beard that went around the yard aggressively defending the fact that he was in prison for fucking his daughter. "I put food in her mouth, so I have a right to put meat in her ass," he was heard to say more than once. So some convicts caught him in his cell one day and when they were through with him he left on a stretcher, still alive but that's the last we saw of him.

Al Doolin put the three guards in an empty cell and made sure they were comfortable, then he posted big Joe Benson in front of their cell, not to keep them in but to keep everybody else out. Me, I noticed a bunch of guys gathered in front of the death row cells and said, "Oh shit," and I headed that direction quickly. We had talked it over, me and Doolin and Poe and the rest of our bunch, and decided that it would be a mistake to mistreat the guards or anybody else, no matter what their crime, because too much was riding on winning this confrontation. Lose, and we'd never see daylight again for a long, long time. Win, and we'd have a release day from the hole, no matter how far away it was. At least we'd know. So this was too serious for fun and games.

I pushed and squeezed my way through the mob and turned to face them with my back against the bars of the death row cells. The leader of the mob was a young, beefy guy with a big jaw and a very loud mouth, so I got face to face with him and spoke before he could figure out what was going on. "Nope, we can't beat up the baby-rapers tonight, another time maybe, but not now."

Well that big dumb fucker, he was befuddled at first. You could see him trying to comprehend what I was saying, see his face turning red. He finally said, "Who the fuck are you?"

I had seen Al Doolin in action enough times to know not to hesitate and I didn't. I popped him right between the eyes as hard as I could. He fell backwards. One of his bunch caught him, and then seeing what he'd caught, let him slide the rest of the way to the floor and looked at me in awe.

"Bill Baker," I said, introducing myself. "Like Al Doolin told you earlier, we are trying to get our hole time set to a definite time. That's too important to risk a bad outcome because we beat up some baby-rapers." I was aware that Al Doolin and Buck Poe had eased up, one on either side of me.

The new speaker of the group, still in awe, said, Oh, Bill Baker—you're one of the Halloween Six guys that escaped from the hole—hey, we weren't going to beat these guys up, we, uh, he (he pointed to the guy who was on the floor trying to get up, shaking his head now) he said these death row guys were homosexuals, so we figured we'd, uh, check 'em out. We've already got definite sentences. I got ten days and he's got ten and thirty."

I just shook my head in disbelief. Al Doolin made up his mind quick, as usual, said, "Okay, take him over to the other side," — talking to the guy with ten days about the guy I'd coldcocked. He added, "All you guys go back to the other side. Well they all looked at each other as if waiting for somebody to say something; when nobody did they straggled back to their own side and Al Doolin locked the door leading into their cell-block. And that solved that problem.

We went back to our side to tend to the captured guards, asked them if they were doing okay, if they needed anything. They had settled down considerably, even engaged in a friendly bullshit session with Joe Benson, who was a master of BS, had a degree in it probably. Big Joe Benson could do two things better than anybody I know: Play pinochle and bullshit. He could maybe even outtalk Buck Poe, except Buck Poe was a legend and he wasn't.

Little Al Brumfield came around the corner and told us the warden was here. That got our attention. Little Al was so quiet by nature that you'd never see him unless you looked real hard, but he'd been with us from the beginning, helped us capture the guards, then he'd gone about halfway up the stairs to stand watch. We'd already called the control room and told them we had their guards captured and that we wanted to see the warden, and now there was already a gang of guards at the top of the stairs on the other side of a locked grill.

So we went around the corner and looked up the stairs and there he was, the warden himself, and he didn't look too happy. At his side was Carl, a new lieutenant who'd brown-nosed his way from a guard in the hole who used to come to work every morning, come back to the back and drink coffee with us and bullshit like he was one of us, he had brown-nosed his was all the way up to the rank of lieutenant in just a few months. When he was working the hole he'd even come back sometimes and take off his shirt and shave, just make himself at home, but we'd figured him as a phony from the very beginning and he was. Now he had his nose up the warden's ass day and night.

I was beginning to almost feel sorry for Warden O'Malley. He must have really been desperate for somebody to support him for him to promote such an obvious phony to lieutenant, but there he was, Lieutenant Carl, at the warden's side. On the warden's other side stood Lieutenant Francis and the old superintendent and several more. They had guns and they definitely did not support the warden's policies in any way shape or form. And, as usual, they wanted to shoot us, which they could have done right then for we were all out there in plain sight, the very convicts they wanted most to shoot, wanted to so badly that they begged the warden right then and there for his permission, and for a minute I felt the hair on the back of my neck prickle for the warden seemed to be seriously considering it. But then he hollered down at us and said, "Where's my guards?" And Al Doolin answered, "They're in a safe place." And the warden said, "Let me see them."

Al Doolin thought about that and then nodded at Buck Poe.

Poe went around the corner and in a few minutes he and Joe Benson came back escorting our captives. They stopped directly behind us, so that we couldn't be shot without hitting the guards too. The warden addressed the guards, asked if any of them had been hurt and when the guards said no the warden asked if they were the only hostages, were there anymore. Assured that we only held those three and no more, the warden asked us what we wanted.

Buck Pope spoke up, explained nicely but firmly that we just wanted to have our hole sentences set to a definite time, that indefinite sentences were too hard to handle, not knowing if we'd ever get out, that the uncertainty of it was not fair, so on and so on until I figured his indefinite speech was not fair either and that the warden might give in to our demands just to shut him up. When he was finally done talking the warden thought about it a long time, then looked at the superintendent and Lieutenant Francis as if inviting their opinion. And that wasn't good.

They both urged him not to give in, that our demands were ridiculous, and that if he, the warden, would give them permission they'd end this standoff real quick. And the warden thought about that, seemed to be considering their words seriously. So we not only had a standoff with the captured guards but we had another drama playing out up there between the new warden and the old regime. Was the warden finally tiring of all the trouble he was having maintaining control of the prison population and with his inability to gain the backing of the old regime? He seemed alone up there, isolated, and his face and posture showed it. It could go either way.

And, I guess Carl, *Lieutenant* Carl, also figured it could go either way for he inched away from the warden's side, sort of eased backwards in preparation to abandon ship if necessary. A subtle move, but I noticed it because I knew Carl.

The warden asked the guards how they were doing, how we had been treating them, maybe just to buy time to think some more before he made a decision. And I'll be damn if one of the guards didn't speak right up, said, "Hey, we were treated real good by all these guys. They laid the law down to everybody else down here not to mess with us and we wound up swapping stories with Joe Benson here (he looked at Benson like he was his best friend or something) and we were just getting ready to play a game of pinochle, the four of us. We were just dealing the cards when you showed up and they brought us out here."

Well I'll be damn, that was just like old Joe Benson, all right.

And that gave the warden something to hang his hat on, I guess, for he straightened up. He was in command again. He asked one more question, addressed it to us: "What about my death row inmates, are they all right?"

I answered that question: "Yep. Nobody messed with them."

I guess he was satisfied with my answer, maybe the tone of my voice, the set of my shoulders, whatever, for he didn't ask to see them or talk to them. He had made up his mind.

He said, "Okay, we'll go get your records and set your sentences. Will you agree to live with the sentences we set and settle down and leave my guards alone?"

I noticed Lieutenant Carl ease back up close to the warden's side. The old superintendent was shaking his head with disappointment. Lieutenant Francis just stared at us with clenched jaw, both hands gripping his gun. He held his tongue with obvious effort.

We thought about the warden's conditions, to live with whatever sentences he set and settle down and leave his guards alone. It was Al Doolin who finally answered. "We'll take the sentences you give us and we'll leave your guards alone, but I can't guarantee we'll be model prisoners. That's a tall order, warden."

"Yes, I suppose it is, for you guys anyway. Okay, you'll take the sentences we set and leave my guards alone for the duration that you remain in the hole under those sentences—" He looked at us and waited for an answer. We agreed quickly to his new wording.

Well, he said it would take a few minutes to dig our files up, but that he'd be back in a little while to set our sentences, and he kept his word. And about three o'clock in the morning sometime around nineteen-fifty-three, I think, in the hole in the state prison in Salem, Oregon, Warden O'Malley held his own court and reset our hole sentences. I came away with five more months to serve, Buck Poe and Al Doolin got seven months, if I remember right, and Joe Benson and the rest got something like six months. I don't remember what Al Brumfield got.

We released the guards, unharmed, and went back to our cells. We had won, but we didn't brag about it, for we were greatly relieved to be able to see the end of our time in the hole at a definite date in the future, and relieved that our siege was over. It had been a close call.

Me, maybe for the first time I began to realize Warden O'Malley was a decent man.

The warden kept his word, and we kept ours. I got out first and immediately took up with my young buddies and we hung out in the vacant building across from the cannery just like old times. Again we were wanted dead or alive by the cannery cops, but to tell the truth I think they enjoyed our games as much as we did for it relieved the boredom of their beat with a little excitement. I say this because they often laughed when we devised some unique tactic that left them embarrassed and bewildered, and when they caught us cold turkey with a counter-plan of their own, they bawled us out triumphantly but then they always turned us loose to try again. They never wrote us up.

I finally decided to sign up for school, just to have something different to do. I took an English class, which I liked a lot and did well in, and I took a science class taught by a wild-eyed convict, which I liked even more, but that didn't last long because the food was getting bad. We had been having issues with the food administrator. For one thing he had fed us a bunch of infected pigs, and a lot of prisoners who ate the pork one day were infected with trichinosis and walked around with pink eyes. One of them died. According to the grapevine, the food administrator was hooked up with the old regime faction led by the superintendent, and they were taking kickbacks from farmers and food vendors and they didn't care how bad the food got, that's what I heard. They wanted to see us have a riot.

The embattled warden was steadily losing support both with the prison guards and with the local newspapers, radio, and television people, thus the general population. There was a strong rumor going around inside the prison that guards and staff who opposed O'Malley—the superintendent and his bunch—were secretly feeding information to the news media, which we figured was true, the rumors, because every time something happened inside the prison that would serve as bad publicity for the warden, the news media announced every detail of it, really played it up big, and they could only have gotten that information from somebody who worked at the prison. So O'Malley, who rode into Salem on a white horse to save civilization, was no longer a hero. His days as warden were numbered. All he had left was the support of Lieutenant Carl (Karl?) and a convict named Punchy Bailey—whose days were also numbered.

Before the big food strike of 'fifty-one the superintendent ran the prison and when O'Malley took over as warden the superintendent was allowed to keep his job, but with reduced authority. That's what we heard, anyway, and the superintendent had been working behind the warden's back ever since to restore himself to power.

Anyway, we had been having problems with the food for some time then, so one day a small riot broke out. It was actually, at first, just a loud demonstration. A mob of convicts gathered on the main prison street and began hollering and raising general hell about the food. Me and my buddies had had nothing to do with starting the demonstration but when we heard all the noise and found out it was about the food we just naturally joined in. It was just a non-violent demonstration and I could holler just as loud as anybody.

But then suddenly out of the rotunda of the main building came, guess who, Lieutenant Francis with a crew of guards armed with tear gas guns, which they immediately began shooting us with. And one of the loads hit somebody right in the face, and that did it. What had been a peaceful demonstration turned into a small but loud prison riot. The prisoner who had been hit in the face was lying on the street screaming, for not only was he blinded by the tear gas but the missile that carried the gas had exploded right in his face at point blank range. Pissed me off. Somewhere I found a wooden stick, not much of a weapon since it was not much bigger than a switch my grandma used to whip me with, but big enough to sting just the same.

A big guard waded in with a fresh load in his gun. He raised it to fire at somebody, again at close range. At that moment I whacked him real good across his wrist and his gun discharged into the street and we both got a good dose of gas.

The demonstration broke up with convicts heading in all directions, so I got the heck out of there too. I made my way into the cell house, took a shower and changed clothes. Afterward I thought nothing about it, figuring it was over. But I guess the guard I'd smacked on the wrist had recognized me and wrote me up, because the next day a bunch of guards came and got me and took me straight to the hole.

And there I was again, but this time they put me on the other side, not on the death row side. I didn't know whether that was an improvement or not.

So I made a lap around my cell, which was all of three and a half long-legged steps each way and then plopped down on my bunk in resignation. But like I said, I was made out of rubber, both in body and spirit and the next day I bounced up and out of my cell ready to take on the world. I ran into a guy in the hole who knew how to make home brew from scratch, without any yeast or sugar or anything, just fruit to get it started. He explained that yeast spores are always present in the air no matter where you are. You don't notice them because they are so tiny and so few, but they are there nevertheless, invisible little yeast cells floating innocently in the air we breathe. And to prove it he, we, saved a bowl of purple plums with thick red juice from breakfast and set it right out in the open with no cover, where it sat for about three days. I watched it and watched it while he lay back on his bunk with confidence, saying don't worry, yeast know how to find fruit, and sure enough he was right, for on the third day tiny gas bubbles started to rise from the plums and by the fourth day it was phizzing like a glass of Alka- Seltzer.

In the meantime we had been saving more fruit and syrup (which had sugar in it he said, the syrup) and so on the fourth night we mixed everything together in a gallon pitcher and set it under the bed to do what yeast and sugar and fruit naturally do when mixed together and left alone, and a few days later we had home brew. It wasn't exactly Tokay wine, but it had alcohol in it. We strained the mixture though a towel and gave five or six guys a shot of it in their cups and we sipped it together and talked. There wasn't enough alcohol in each portion to give anybody more than a mild buzz, but it tasted good. It tasted like, uh, fruit juice.

He, the yeast scientist, said all I had to do now was save the squeezings from the towel and use that as a kicker for the next batch, so on and so forth, home brew forever. So that's what I did, started a forever-and-ever winery. I didn't drink much of it. I had learned long ago that I didn't have any special desire for alcohol of any kind, but it was fun making it—well, no, the fun was in getting away with making it, for there was enough risk in making it to get the adrenalin going. I got caught as often as I got away with it, which made it worth it. Does that make any sense?

Fermenting brew gives off a strong yeasty-fruity smell, a smell distinct from every other smell if you have a nose for it. And a guard called Frenchy, who was working the hole at the time, had a nose for it. He could smell fermenting brew a mile away through mop water with a gallon of pine oil in it and baby powder and after-shave lotion sprinkled from one end of the hole to the other, Frenchy could still smell it. And his nose led him straight to it.

Frenchy was a legend of a rare kind in the Oregon State Prison. First, he was as ugly as a humpback frog, short and squat with a big head, a dark blemished face and an enormous nose. He had worked at the prison forever, they say, and had survived the big food strike and the change in wardens without a care in the world for who was in charge. All he wanted to do was do his job and draw his paycheck and go home at night and come back to work the next day. Nobody knew what he went home to, but he always went home dirty, because they always gave him the dirtiest jobs, which he did without complaint, and he came to work clean the next day, that's all anybody knew about his home life. He was, they say, incredibly stupid, and in all the years he worked only got a few minor promotions.

He was too stupid to be afraid, which he often proved by wading right into the middle of a fight or riot, with or without backup, and he should have been killed a thousand times but wasn't. How he had survived nobody knew. They cussed him out daily, especially when he found their stash of home brew and poured it out right in front of them. They cussed and cussed till their faces turned purple, but he paid no attention to words, just kept right on pouring the fruits of their hard labor into Shit Creek. Once he even jumped right into Shit Creek himself when a convict he was searching threw a sack of dope into the creek to keep from getting caught with it. Well Frenchy did a belly flop right into the creek and waded out stinking, but he had that sack of dope in is hand.

One thing that may have saved him from getting stabbed full of holes is that he didn't take it personal when he got cussed out, and he seldom wrote a disciplinary report on anybody. He just did his job, no matter what, and then went on about his business. He often had a remorseful look on his face when he poured out somebody's wine. He obviously didn't get a kick out of it like some guards did.

Anyway, Frenchy could smell home brew a mile away and he was working the hole just when I had the urge to open a brewery in that same hole he was working in. And that presented a challenge that kept me busy for most of the time I spent in the hole. I tried everything to hide the smell. I hid it in garbage cans underneath the most stinking garbage imaginable. He found it, poured it down the toilet. I cussed him out. The next time I took the screen out of the exhaust vent in the back of my cell and hung it in the utility corridor, put the screen back in place. He found it, poured it down the toilet. I cussed him out. The next time I set up two batches, one where it would be easy for him to smell and then find, and the other a few feet from it but completely hidden, and I started them fermenting on the first of his two days off so that when he came back he would only have one day to find it before we strained it and drank it. When he came back to work sure enough he found the decoy, poured it down the toilet. I cussed him out. The decoy would smell up the place for another day and he would smell that as well as the hidden batch and not know the difference. That time we got him.

The next day we drank the fresh batch of brew with the extra pleasure of knowing we had finally tricked old Frenchy's nose. And we used the same method several more times with success, but then I made a mistake. When he poured out the brew in our decoy I forgot to cuss him out, so pleased was I with myself. Well he looked at me with those big remorseful eyes, as usual, but he knew something was wrong for he was accustomed to getting cussed out when he poured out somebody's wine. He was slow and it took him a while to figure it out, but he came by my cell sniffing three or four times and then a light must have gone on in his brain and he came in my cell and sniffed again and then he tore up my cell like a dog digging for a mole. And he found it. Poured it down the toilet. And I cussed him out properly this time.

He slowed me down for a few days, but I always kept a kicker in a small jar so I could start a new batch and so I did just that. I mixed up a batch and hung it on the bars outside the window and covered it with a wet T-shirt like I was drying the shirt in the fresh air and then I closed the window. He would never be able to smell that. But he did. Some idiot came along and opened the window to get some fresh air and old Frenchy got a good whiff of it and followed his nose straight to it. Just like that.

So we won some and lost some, but it was something to do to break up the monotony.

Then one day Frenchy didn't come to work and we asked what had happened to him, and the new guard said they'd assigned him to a new job on the shake-down crew on the yard. And we rejoiced at our good fortune. But the new guard was so easy it wasn't much fun anymore. To tell the truth I sort of missed old Frenchy.

After that the days slowed down to life in the slow lane, and then one day they stopped altogether. No one knew what was happening but there was no water in the sink or toilet, our doors didn't open for rec, and there was no guard in the hole. And when it was time for chow the chow cart didn't show up. And when it was time for supper the chow cart didn't show up again, nor any guards nor any word from anybody. The cell house above us was completely silent, too, whereas you could always hear some kind of sound coming from it. I mean it was like something out of a ghost story.

That night my mouth and throat got dry from lack of water, but I was able to sleep anyway. The next morning came and still no water, no guards, no food. Then things really got serious for I ran out of tobacco, we all ran out of tobacco, every one of us, though I think somebody was holding out because I smelled smoke coming from both sides of me.

Finally a guard came through counting, and he was moving fast. When we asked him what was going on and where was everybody and what happened to the water—everybody talking at once—all he said was everybody was on the yard, and he kept on moving.

So it didn't take a genius to figure out that something real serious was going down.

Late that same day some guards showed up and immediately began unlocking our doors, all our doors. "Get out of here, you're free," one of them hollered without slowing down. He didn't have to tell me twice, I took off like a jackrabbit scared out of a bush, up the stairs I went, out the cell house door, through the rotunda and out the back door to the street, skidded to a stop in front of the commissary. The metal door was wide open and commissary was scattered all over the place behind the counter, cookies, candy, all kinds of goodies, I mean zoo-zoo's and wham-wham's everywhere, and soda pop too. I quickly gathered up an arm-load and headed for the sawdust bin where I plopped down and ate and drank till my belly was about to pop. And I still had not seen or heard a convict or guard anywhere.

Eventually I wandered back through the deserted rotunda and into a cell house. All doors were wide open. I came to an unbelieving stop when I saw the mess in front of me inside the cell house. The wide corridor in front of the cells was piled high with the personal property of the convicts who lived in the cell house. It was all mixed together and scattered about like a hurricane had hit, pictures, letters, books, a busted guitar, just piles and piles of litter from the cells. All the cells had been cleaned out completely, all the way to the top tier, with nothing left but a mattress and a roll of toilet paper. That meant the guards had done it, cleaned everything out of all the cells and thrown it all over the tier as they went.

In a little while I heard something going on and I peeped out the cell house door and saw a bunch of guards escorting a bunch of handcuffed convicts through the rotunda to the hole. They had turned us loose to make room for them.

My freedom lasted for one night. The next day they gathered me up along with about fifty more guys who were considered troublemakers and locked us all up on the bottom range of one of the cell houses, and that's where we stayed, our new home, no explanation or anything.

In the days that followed I pieced together what had happened. First, we had a new warden. He was an old gimp-legged warden from the federal prison system. I don't remember his name because we just mainly called him The Gimp or Gimpy or whatever, behind his back of course for to call him Gimpy to his face was suicide as we found out early when an unknowing convict called him Gimpy. When the convict got out of the hole he was older and wiser. The Gimp didn't take no shit.

They had had a big riot on the yard. And the people of Oregon had had enough. It was time to put a stop to the goings on at the prison, the riots and strikes and such. O'Malley had to go. So the state police took control, lined the wall with state troopers and herded every single prisoner, except the guys locked in the hole, onto the yard and made them all get down on the ground on their belly and stay there. And stay there they did, for every time one of them moved a shot was fired from a trooper on the wall and the convict's body was sprayed with dirt from a bullet that barely missed him. It was a hot sunny day and there was no water. All the water inside the institution had been turned off. The heat became unbearable as it soaked the moisture from the air and from the human bodies on the ground. And the next day, when it was over, the prisoners were only too glad to go back to a cell and be locked down in a cell barren of everything except a mattress and a roll of toilet paper, and those who were put in the hole were glad to go there too, anywhere as long as there was water.

Anyway, they rounded up all the troublemakers and locked us down, whether we had been in the riot or not, and we stayed there on the bottom range of one of the cell houses until they opened up the new segregation building which had just been completed. It was all steel and concrete with bars of hardened steel that couldn't be cut with hacksaw blades. They put me in a single cell on the second floor, which was the segregation section. We never got out of our cells for rec and if we caused trouble they had something special for us on the first floor. I had to try it out of course. That was my nature. And I found myself in a dark cell in the back of the first floor. The cell contained nothing, absolutely nothing, no bunk, no toilet, no sink, just four walls and a hole in the floor. They came with a jug of water once or twice a day—no food. Every third day they moved me to a cell in the front section and fed me three regular meals, and then moved me back to the dark cell for another stay. That lasted for about nine days, I think, and I didn't like it very much. That was the new hole.

When they moved me back upstairs they kept me there another couple of months and then one day came and cut me loose back into population.

The new warden was in complete control by now. The first thing he'd done was get rid of Punchy Bailey, boarded him out on a one way trip to Alcatraz. The next thing he'd done was fire everybody who might oppose his authority and cause him problems in the future, and that included the old superintendent who'd been so instrumental in getting O'Malley fired and who wasn't even finished celebrating his victory. The Gimp was no fool. He'd brought his own staff with him, people he could trust. Lieutenant Francis, however, had survived the new warden's purge. How, I don't know.

As for the prisoners, they had settled down to normal prison life in what was a normal prison now: everybody had a job doing something, even if it was just polishing door knobs. We probably had the cleanest door knobs in the world. Me, I bought an old acoustic guitar on credit from a guy who had decided learning to play a guitar was hard work and not at all like his five-easy-lessons book had advertised. I'd been fooling with a guitar off and on since reform school so before long I was playing in the prison band. I also signed up for school again to get out of working in the mess hall.

And weekends and evenings I walked the yard alone. My old buddies, Pomroy and Hopper and the General, all had jobs and had settled into their separate routines. I ran into Buck Poe and Al Doolin and Joe Benson once in a while out sunning themselves or pitching horseshoes or playing dominoes, never together for they had gone their separate ways. I stopped to talk about old times, but they didn't seem to have much enthusiasm for that so a quick wave as I passed them by became the norm. They had been completely pasture-ized, I guess.

But at age eighteen I still yearned for adventure, and true to form the Gimp had built fences everywhere, a fence around the big yard, a fence that cut off the cannery from inmate access, a fence here a fence there a fence everywhere. So I rode the trails with Zane Grey at night in my cell and wandered the yard alone with my head in the air thinking about this and that and space and time, but I kept running into the "f" word, "forever," which seemed to me to apply equally to both space and time in a way that I couldn't understand but which was maybe my first crude inkling of the concept of spacetime. But I always wound up with a sprained brain when I ran into "forever," so riding the purple sage with Zane Grey was a welcome relief, and more my speed.

But I wasn't finished. I still yearned for excitement. And one day my chance came, a chance for my star-spangled swan song, my final goodbye to Oregon. And I went out with a splash. It was a hot day. I was on the little yard watching the card games. Toilet buckets were no longer dumped into Shit Creek because the old cell house that had no toilets had been torn down and replaced with a new one that did.

So I looked at the waters of Shit Creek and got a sudden urge. And the next thing I knew I was coming out of my clothes. Then I dove into Shit Creek head first and went for one hell of a swim. I was aware of the bull horn in the guard tower hollering an alarm, but I paid no attention for I was having a good old time, splashing up a storm. And I was aware of convicts along the bank cheering me along. And when I was finished and climbed up the bank dripping wet I was aware of old Frenchy standing there with an amazed look on his face as he watched me emerge buck naked.

So me, I stood up straight with my ding dongs dangling in the wind and saluted him with a hand to the forehead like a true red-blooded American convict. Just like that. Frenchy turned about ten colors, and for a minute I thought he was going to have a heart attack, but then he just let out a laugh, shook his head and walked away.

Maybe it wasn't a big deal, that swim, but I'll always

remember it. And I can't say it was any kind of religious experience or anything like that, I don't know. But my brother, the Reverend R.D. Baker, had travelled all the way to Jerusalem to contemplate the sacred waters of the Sea of Galilee. Me, I swam in Shit Creek.

And I got out of the Oregon State Penitentiary and went to Denty Moore's Tavern and met Signey Meeker, who relieved me of my burden, after which I cast a taller shadow on the land on my way to Alcatraz.

*****

CHAPTER FIFTEEN

Me and Burgett were doing pushups on the yard, well, he was doing pushups, I was mostly watching, though I did a few just to entertain Jack Waites and Fat Duncan, who were out of the hole again, and Benny Rayburn, who bet me I couldn't do twenty. So I plopped down and knocked out thirty and bounced back up like they weren't nothing. Fat Duncan laughed, and turned to Benny Rayburn. "I knew he was going to win that bet. Anybody that's done a lot of hole time knows how to do pushups. Now why don't you drop down and give us twenty yourself, Benny Rayburn?"

Benny grinned, said he couldn't do pushups and wasn't about to go to the hole to learn.

Burgett said to me, "Hey, hit me in the belly." And he stood there straight with his arms wide to present a good target." I knew he was toughening up for his big swim, so I punched him in the belly but not too hard.

"Hit me harder," he said.

"Let me hit him," Jack Waites volunteered.

Burgett just laughed, said, "You haven't got enough ass to knock me off the spot I'm standing on, Jack Waites." And I thought Burgett was probably right for Jack was even skinnier that I was, and not as tall. But Jack took the bet, stood up and punched him as hard as he could. Burgett flinched a little but his feet didn't move an inch.

Well old Simmons, the little young guard who had been messing with everybody, must have been watching for he came running, came to a stop between Jack and Burgett. "Break it up!" he hollered. Surprised the hell out of everybody. Burgett just laughed and said, "No, we weren't fighting, I asked him to punch me in the stomach to tighten it up." And Burgett pounded on his stomach with a fist to show how hard it was.

Simmons didn't want to give up, and for a minute he stood there red-faced and undecided, then he said, "Well horseplay is against the rules, too. Someone could get hurt or someone might get mad and start a fight. I saw Baker hit you in the stomach and I saw Waites hit you, and I know what I saw and I'm notifying you right now that if I see it again I'm writing you up, all of you." With those words of warning he retreated down the steps, and as he did Fat Duncan let out a loud mouth fart that stiffened his back and turned his face redder than it already was but he kept on going.

Fat Duncan and Jack Waites were just a few years older than me, and both of them were good guys but they could get crazy as hell sometimes, like the time they both cut their heel strings in protest over conditions in the hole or something, which was further proof that they were quality convicts, though maybe not as smart as some. They had spent about as much time in jails as I had, judging from the way they talked.

Jack Waites was in for bank robbery. I don't remember what Fat Duncan was in for. He didn't talk much about his past.

Fat Duncan was jolly and talkative most of the time, but he had his times of deep silence too, and you knew there was a lot of pain there somewhere. When he was out of the hole there were times when he wouldn't come out of his cell, even to go eat, and I saw Jack Waites carry him a sandwich or something back from the mess hall more than once. One day I asked Jack about it and he just shrugged and said, "He's all right, he's just doing some hard time right now.

As for Jack, he was a pretty steady guy, talked a lot but didn't laugh and joke a lot. He was a real hard-head and a real convict.

In later years I saw Fat Duncan in the U. S. Penitentiary in Atlanta, Georgia, where he had been transferred when they closed down Alcatraz. Duncan went to the hole by his own request shortly after he got there because he couldn't stand the wide open population of Atlanta and the big eight-man or ten-man cells. When I talked to him he was temporarily in the prison hospital in a private cell. He told me he was on thorazine. He said they had repeatedly offered to turn him out of the hole but he said he'd spent so much time in the hole in Alcatraz that he'd been conditioned to the confined space and now he couldn't stand wide-open spaces. He was real humble when he talked about it, and despite being heavily medicated he talked rationally and honestly. It was really sad, but I guess a lot of time in the hole does that to some people.

That's the last I saw of him. He went back to the hole and committed suicide.

As for Jack Waites, I saw him too in later years, and he too was in the hospital, but he was in the TB. ward and he hadn't changed a bit. He was back in prison after a brief but colorful run in which he and some of his buddies, of which he had hundreds by now for everybody knew Jack Waites, he and some of his buddies went down to Alabama and broke another buddy out of the brand-new escape-proof jail in Selma. It was a spectacular event in which he and all his buddies, and anyone who even remotely looked like any of them, were wanted by every law enforcement agency in the land and especially by the sheriff of Dallas County, upon which land the previously unescapable jail had been built, wanted every last one of them dead or alive but mostly dead.

That was Jack Waites.

And I drove past that jail one day on my way to a fresh check-cashing territory and remembered him. The jail was out in the country, had a high security fence around it and everything. It must have been a hard jail to crack.

Jack Waites did a lot of time but he died free. He died of TB on the streets of Atlanta.

At Alcatraz, with Jack Waites and Fat Duncan out of the hole, we had enough players to make up a team for a softball game, so one Sunday afternoon that's what we did, and we played Punchy Bailey's team and were sure to lose but we didn't care, we were just goofing off as usual. There was me and Waites and Duncan and Benny Rayburn and Forest Tucker and Burgett and Clyde Johnson and somebody else. Even though we didn't know Clyde all that well, he and Burgett had become good friends so we asked him to play with us. That he and Burgett were planning to escape together, I had no doubt, but I never brought it up and neither did they.

We took the field and, as usual, we got two or three runs behind right away, just goofing off having fun. Simmons and Lieutenant Mitchell were watching from the sidelines over by first base, and Simmons seemed to be having fun watching us get beat up, so we figured it would be a great opportunity to exact a little revenge, nothing serious but just a little something for him to think about, whereupon we made up a little plot which Fat Duncan begged to be the primary weapon of. No problem, upon his next time at bat Fat Duncan took a mighty swing at the ball and as usual the ball dribbled down the third base line at a leisurely roll and Duncan took off for first base. He got up a pretty good head of steam, too, lumbering across the base at break-neck speed considering how heavy he was. And, as everybody knows, the heavier the object the harder it is to stop. Fat Duncan thundered well past the base, tried to make the turn like other runners did, but momentum and weight wouldn't let him. Instead his feet got tangled up and he careened sideways and ran smack-dab into Officer Simmons belly first, knocked poor Simmons clean off his feet and flat on his back. And Duncan landed right on top of him.

Lieutenant Mitchell, Fat Mitchell, didn't know what to think, but he was quick to react, as usual, pulled Duncan off the flattened officer with a mighty heave. Simmons just lay there like he'd been run over by a tractor-trailer. He gagged for breath, his face was death white.

What did Duncan do? He apologized as he offered Simmons his hand to help him up, said all kinds of "Sorry, I couldn't stop, I tripped, I didn't see you there," all the while extending his hand to help the poor Simmons off the ground. Simmons got up all right, with the help of Fat Mitchell—he wouldn't take Duncan's hand for all the money in the world.

Duncan explained to Fat Mitchell that it was just an accident, which it had certainly seemed to be, and the game resumed with little delay, no harm intended. But the whole yard cracked up laughing and cheering when it happened and Simmons glared poison arrows at us the rest of the game. Somehow he knew he'd been had.

And that wasn't the only bit of revenge we exacted that day.

Punch Bailey's usual mild and friendly manner often changed during a softball game, or any competitive sport or game. He could really get aggressive, sometimes too aggressive. And for some reason he chose to talk a little too much shit with us that day. All we were doing was having some fun bumbling around on the field like a bunch of bums, which is what we were. It didn't matter whether we won or not. But Punchy Bailey kept chiding us to the point of being downright mean-spirited. We overlooked it for a while, but then he went a little too far and the disrespect in his words was obvious to us and anybody watching the game. Enough.

Pissed off, we huddled before the next inning. "Let's win this fucking game," I said. "Burgett, knock the hell out of the ball, but don't knock it over the wall." Knocking the ball over the wall was an automatic out at Alcatraz, I guess because the yard was so little and of course we couldn't go over the wall to find balls that went over. The guards had to do that, so the rule at Alcatraz was a ball over the wall was not a home run but an out instead.

Anyway, we came to bat with determination on our faces.

Burgett knocked five homeruns that day, driving them all the way to the far end to scatter the handball players or high on the bleachers where they bounced off buildings and steps so unpredictably that it took forever to recover a ball, and the rest of us managed to hold our own, so we beat the heck out of old Punchy Bailey's sacred softball team.

And that shut Punchy Bailey up for a while. After the game he had a sober look on his face. He, too, knew he had been had.

And the next weekend Burgett died in the San Francisco Bay.

Before he left he gave me some cigarettes and things he had in his stash, and he shook my hand, said, "No use getting this stuff wet." That's all he said. But I knew what he meant. And that weekend him and Clyde Johnson captured the garbage truck guard, bound him, and hit the water.

We first knew about it when they locked us down. The radio cop tried to censor it out of the news, but it was a waste of his time for the escape was all that was talked about on the local radio stations. They had caught Clyde Johnson clinging to a rock out on Little Alcatraz, but Burgett was nowhere to be found. Clyde Johnson was crying when they spotted him, so I knew what had happened but I hoped otherwise. In later years some bonehead prison guard reported that when they captured Clyde Johnson he was crying and clinging to that rock like a sniveling coward, and that report became part of the historical record of the escape. But I can tell you for certain that that report is pure bullshit, and something only a prison guard would say, for I knew Clyde Johnson for many years both at Alcatraz and Leavenworth, and Clyde Johnson was no coward. He was crying because he had just witnessed his partner die in those churning waters. And if you can't cry when you see your best buddy die then shame on you; I sure wouldn't want to be in a foxhole with you.

We were locked down for about ten days I think, though I don't remember for sure. Maybe it was only a week but it seemed like forever. I could look out the window and see the search boat circling the island day and night, see its spotlight probing the darkness at night, and that gave us some hope. I walked the floor and read some books, I even read *The Old Man and the Sea*, a book by Hemmingway that I had started to read many times but hadn't made it past the first few pages. The book made a big fuss about a fish but I made it through it and remembered it long after the dust settled in the Old West. It was a book of struggle and hope and final triumph. It was the book I read when Burgett died.

Then one day they opened our doors and the prison returned to normal operation. They had found Burgett's body washed up in one of the holes the sea had carved into the island's shore. They found his body but his soul was long gone.

And free of that cell my spirit returned to normal operation, as it always did, being made of Rubbermaid and all that. I once again challenged Jackrabbit to a game of bridge. Me and my partner had a secret weapon this time. We had a book by the rising authority on the game of bridge, Charles Goren. He had written that book in simple language that anybody could understand, including me. It was more geared to my generation, I figured, not Jackrabbit's old fuddy-duddy Eli Culbertson generation. I was twenty-three years old and pretty pleased with myself.

Well, the game was on. When we settled down to the card table, I remember how Jackrabbit looked his calm confident self, probably figuring we weren't worthy of any worry on his part, that I was the same old pushover, la de da de and all that, but I had something for his old ass this time. I tried not to snicker.

As is the rule in a bridge game each pair of players has to declare what bidding system they are using, and any special bids, slam invitation bids, so on and so forth. When I said

Charles Goren I was super cool about it, just sort of nonchalantly threw it out there.

Jackrabbit nodded, didn't seem overly impressed, and the game began.

And again he tore my young ass up one side and down the other, completely fucked me up. I don't remember the final score, but I remember it wasn't pretty. And when it was over I stood up and said, "Damn, Jackrabbit!" And I headed for the other end of the yard with my tail between my legs.

I remember that very well.

One day I was sitting up on the bleachers and Jackrabbit came by with a homemade birthday card in his hand, said, "Sign this for Forest Tucker. His birthday's coming up." And he handed the card to me along with a pen to sign it with. It was a real pretty card with a bunch of designs and a big "Happy Birthday, Forest Tucker" on it which must have taken a lot of painstaking work to make. On the back of it was already a bunch of signatures. A lot of people liked Forest Tucker. I wrote a "Happy Birthday" on it and signed my name.

"When is your birthday?" Jackrabbit asked me. Alarmed, I answered quickly to head him off. "Naw, Jackrabbit. I don't have birthdays. Forget about that."

He shrugged, seemed satisfied with my answer. But just to make sure I said, "A birthday is just another day."

"Okay," he said. And we talked awhile about other things. He said the new metal detector had come in. They'd unloaded it on the dock and would start construction on the shack to house it within the next couple of weeks. "They're going to put it on the landing on the way down the steps to the factory."

When we were finished talking Jackrabbit left to get more signatures, but before he left he asked, "How old are you?" Just sort of slipped it in sideways.

"Twenty-three," I answered sadly.

*****

CHAPTER SIXTEEN

We all gathered around as Jackrabbit gave the "surprised" Forest Tucker his birthday card, let him read it first, and then presented him with a sack of goodies Benny Rayburn had "secretly" collected from close friends. I contributed three precious cigars to the collection. Last Christmas they had put six cigars in our Christmas bags, and cigars were too precious and worth too much money to smoke, so I still had three of mine, well, I had none now. Somebody had put a bag of hard candy in the gift sack, and there were nuts and other goodies too. Forest Tucker had the biggest grin on his face I'd ever seen in my life as he read the card and pulled goodies from the bag, man, what a grin he had. You'd think he was a little kid the way he grinned and carried on. Maybe we were all a bunch of little kids, for we all enjoyed it as much as he, I think. After we milked all the joy out of it we could, we sat around and sucked on hard candy with Forest Tucker and felt good.

I had nothing against birthdays, they were good; they just weren't for me. All the fuss embarrassed me. I used to have good birthdays when my grandma was alive. They were fun then, all the attention I got, and the presents, especially the presents, but the love too when all was said and done and I crawled up in my grandma's lap and went to sleep against her soft ample bosom.

I remember when I was seven or eight that the only problem I had with life was trying to figure out which end of a girl was up.

Then my grandma died and my mother came after me and I hid in the closet when I saw the strange car coming down the dusty road to get me, which did no good, the closet, for they found me and I met those big old clod-hopper shoes from which my big old step dad grew upward from. Zeb Hackney. He was a tall, big-boned man with a shiny bald head. He was twelve years older than my mother, but it was those shoes that first caught my attention and which I still remember well to this day, for he planted each one of them in my ass a whole bunch of times in the years to come. He believed in swift retribution, Old Testament style. Never mind a switch when a boot was handy. And before you think I'm whining about it, I'll admit right now that I deserved his swift justice most of the time. I wasn't exactly a model kid like Jack, my younger brother, when I was growing up.

Anyway, my mother and Zeb Hackney with those clod-hopper boots found me hiding in the closet and took me away to Hackney Land.

And right away when my mother tried to hug and pet on me I let her know I was off-limits. I squirmed out of her arms real quick. And the next time she tried it I pulled away so violently that she never tried it again. It wasn't that I felt any hate for her, or anything like that, it was just that it was embarrassing, this strange woman fussing over me like that. I couldn't stand it. And for many years, until it was almost too late, I never once called her Mama or Mother or any of those mushy names kids call their mothers—until she lay dying in a nursing home and I realized how much I would miss her when she was gone.

She didn't love me and I didn't love her, and we both knew it, but she was always there, there somewhere in my Being, in the background of my soul, maybe, I don't know. I just know she was always there. And through all my years on the road and all my years in prisons and jails, even though we hardly ever wrote, a card here a letter there with long lapses in between, I still knew she was there.

Hackney Land wasn't a bad land for those who belonged in it, I guess. Everybody said Zeb Hackney was a good man, worked hard, went to church, had an obedient wife. It's just that from the very beginning I knew I didn't belong there. I was a round sapling that didn't fit in the square world that was the Land of Hackney.

Hackney Land covered a hundred and twenty acres of tree-covered hills and rich bottom lands in Southwestern Kentucky. Zeb was a farmer in a time when small farms fed the nation, long before corporate farming came along and put small farmers out of business. People lived on their farms back then, and they grew their own food in fields and gardens and raised their own pigs and cows and chickens. They killed their pigs and smoked the meat and salted the bacon for the long haul, because folks in the country didn't have refrigerators back then. They didn't even have electricity. And they milked their own cows for milk and butter and cream. The chickens laid eggs, and as was their fate in life, a good chicken dinner was always just a neck-wringing away, happily pecking its last meal in the back yard.

Once in a while we took some chickens to town and sold them for cash, but mostly we just carried cream, which we separated from milk in a hand-cranked separator, and eggs, which the chickens laid in nests in the hen house without any help from us, we took the cream and eggs over to the country store in Walnut Grove and traded them for flour and sugar and other things we needed. The barter system—that's the way business was done in Hackney Land, and I'm not complaining about that, for we ate good. Zeb Hackney put food on the table every day of the year, and he sent me to school and bought shoes for my rapidly growing feet every winter, and he let me go barefooted and run wild all summer long, so he did his part, everything required by law.

And the milk, we drank it just like it came out of the cow, rich in cream and natural goodness, real *whole* milk, not the fake whole milk you get in a super market today with most of the cream and other nutrients extracted for other money-making products so that what you get is mostly milk-colored water, we drank real milk right out of Old Bessie. That it was not Pasteurized and therefore filled with germs fortunately never occurred to us. I say fortunately because by drinking un-Pasteurized milk we became immune to every enteric bacteria known to man, including salmonella.

What does milk have to do with anything? Nothing. But if you're thinking about going into hot checks as a criminal career you might ought to toughen up your immune system so you can eat a lot of rotten prison food.

I thought I'd just throw that in.

Anyway, when I was first taken to Hackney Land we stayed with some of Zeb Hackney's relatives, because his house was not yet built. And we went to Detroit where both he and my mother worked in factories that had been geared up for the war effort. There I went to school and eventually learned how to play hooky. I did very well at that, playing hooky. With my little brother often in tow, I roamed the streets of Detroit looking for bandits and hidden treasure in abandoned buildings, every day a great adventure of discovery, of sights and sounds different from anything I'd ever imagined.

When I was supposed to be in school I was seldom there, and when I was there I still wasn't there for my mind was elsewhere. One day it was raining so I went to school to get out of the rain, at least I had sense enough to do that. Well, it just so happened that on that day they had a school-wide spelling bee, and it was a big school with a lot of contestants. Me, I was prodded up on stage when it was my turn and they started giving me words to spell and I spelled them unconsciously, without a clue as to what I was doing. And I won.

I won the whole thing to the applause of many students and the bafflement of many teachers. And I received as a prize a new dictionary from the Detroit News with my name printed in gold on the front cover. And the next day after the spelling bee the skies cleared and I was gone again.

Eventually a teacher sent a dirty note to my mother wanting to know why I was never in school, but I was able to lie out of that because my mother had just received my new dictionary with my name printed in gold, along with a letter of congratulations from the powerful Detroit News for winning the spelling bee, which I had already forgotten about. It came just in time to save me. When I say save me I mean I wasn't worried about my mother whipping me, for I was, like I said, off-limits to her, and that included whippings. But she sometimes, if my transgressions were serious enough, handed me over to a higher power, meaning my stepfather, Zeb Hackney, who was lethal with a belt or his big leather razor strop, whichever one was handiest. He had not yet learned to kick me with those clodhoppers, which he wore even in Detroit.

Anyway, I started running away from home when I was nine or ten. The first time was on the exact day that the big race riot started in Bell Isle Park and spread quickly to the whole city of Detroit. I planned to walk out into the countryside and camp like a cowboy. I said goodbye to my little brother, who cried when I left, but cowboys have to move on, so I took off down the street with a spring in my step on a brand new adventure. I stopped at a store and bought a box of matches, which I'd need to start a campfire with, and continued on my merry way—and continued and continued, for Detroit was a lot bigger than I had ever imagined. I stopped for a while to rest my horse, I mean a cowboy has to rest his horse once in a while, and feed it too. I bought enough candy for both me and my horse, but my horse wasn't hungry so I ate his too.

Night came and I was still walking. On and on I went. Later and later it got. I noticed a lot of black men running around turning over cars and setting fires. It was a colorful sight and I stopped to watch for a bit, then I moved on down the sidewalk. Some of the blacks noticed me but they didn't bother me and I continued on until it was time to water my horse, so I walked into a bar to ask for water, but the bartender got real excited about me walking around the streets in the middle of a race riot—that's what he called it, a race riot—and when I told him I was headed to the country to camp out and just needed some water, he called the police.

The police took me to a big jail somewhere, and when I wouldn't give them my name or address they put me in a cell, the first jail cell I'd ever been in, and I went straight to sleep. The trail takes a toll on a cowboy.

I guess my mother notified the police that I'd run away because sometime during the night she came and got me, my mother did. As far as I was concerned she could have let me sleep.

That wasn't the last time I ran away. Once I got the taste of the wild blue yonder, I took off every time the urge struck me, staying at home just long enough to fill my belly a few times and catch up on my sleep. Once I even made it to Chicago. But the folks of that city didn't appreciate a ten-year-old kid running around stealing jugs of milk off back porches or fresh-baked pies set to cool in open windows. Nor did they appreciate me sleeping in the back seat of a car and then playing dead when the young driver came out of the house and reached into the back of that car in the dark for something he had forgotten and felt my shoe and then my leg and then my knee, groping in the dark to identify the strange object he had encountered. He identified it. He let out a scream and took off running.

Me, I came out of that car and took off running in the opposite direction, just as scared as he was, I think. The police found me hiding in a garage and took me to jail, where I remained until my mother came after me and took me back to Detroit on a bus. She wasn't too happy with me, nor was my step father who welcomed me home with a razor strop to my backside. He wasn't mad because I'd run away from home, he was mad because my mother had had to miss two days of work to go to Chicago to get me.

Sometime after that we moved back to Hackney Land and lived with some of Zeb's folks while he built his house. He built it from the ground up with his own hands, I'll give him credit for that. He cut down trees and dragged the logs behind a horse to an old one-man sawmill he'd bought from somebody, and sawed those logs into planks of all sizes and thicknesses and built that house from the ground up with his own hands—well mostly his own hands, I helped some.

He introduced me to Work. I didn't like that a lot. So he introduced me to his clodhoppers up my ass. I liked that even less. So I Worked.

When he finished building his house, we moved in, me and my brother in one bedroom and he and my mother in the other. The house had a living room with a fire place and a picture window, and it had a kitchen. Zeb established himself on a chair in the living room in front of the fireplace and from there he ruled Hackney Land, and rule it he did. My mother wilted into a submissive housewife under his dominant will, for that was the way of women in Hackney Land, all women, the part they played in the lives of men in that time and place. And my mother accepted that role willingly and peacefully, even happily. She cooked the food, cleaned the house, and worked in the garden. In her spare time she read romance stories and dreamed of the time when my father, Garnet Baker, would come riding in to rescue her. Her favorite country song was *Chained to a Memory of You* by somebody, I don't remember who, and she sometimes went about her housework humming that song.

Zeb worked a lot, either on the farm or on construction jobs here and there, so he was gone a lot during the day. I liked that, him being gone. But when he came home he cast a gray shadow over the whole house that nobody noticed except me. Jack didn't notice it. My mother didn't notice it. But I did. I stayed out of the house most of the time he was there.

It wasn't my house anyway, no part of it, and it certainly wasn't my home. If I was making a movie about that time in my life I'd name it Homeless in Hackney Land. And there'd be sad violins playing in the background, but maybe a fiddle, too, frolicking faintly from somewhere, for it would be a soap opera and a comedy too and would bring tears and laughter at the same time—if I was making a movie.

I started running away again, and not because anybody mistreated me, I just had a taste for adventure and I found that on the road. I hitchhiked all over Kentucky, stopping at a relative's house for a meal or a night's sleep now and then. I had relatives on the Baker's side all over the state and other states as well. A ride was easy to come by in those days, those days when people picked up hitchhikers, those days before cigarettes caused cancer or asbestos caused a name I can't pronounce, those days when a drink of water was free in all gas stations and there were no tornadoes or hurricanes or earthquakes unless one smacked into you personally, for they had no televisions in those days to tell you about them so vividly and persistently, therefore they didn't exist.

And if you couldn't find a gas station for a drink of water all you had to do was plop on your belly at any small stream and drink till your belly was full, those days when the water was clear and clean.

But they had jails in those days, too, and that's where I often wound up.

Finally, when I was about eleven or twelve years old, I wound up in a jail in my hometown of Princeton and Zeb Hackney had had enough. He told my mother to have me committed to a reform school, which she obligingly did. And early the next morning after the papers were signed they whisked me off to the Greendale Reformatory outside of Frankfort, Kentucky.

I stayed there for thirteen long months, during which time I learned to smoke cigarettes, fight, and dislike the sorry reform school guards.

167

When I got there they had just outlawed the blacksnake whip because a young kid had died from a brutal whipping by a reform school guard. It happened though that the kid's relatives had a little money, enough to pay a lawyer and as a result of a public hearing there was a big stink, so—no more blacksnake whips. They were replaced by paddles. The paddles were about three feet long and four inches wide and a half inch thick with five or six half-inch holes bored through the paddle end to produce more sting. And for punishment you had to bend over a bench and take five or ten or twenty whacks across your ass, sometimes delivered by a guard and sometimes an older inmate who had been promoted to house boy in the absence of a guard. It was the inmate house boys who delivered the most vicious blows.

If you could bend over and "ride" ten whacks without a whimper you were a man and most of us could do that though it hurt like hell. I remember, though, that there was one young blond boy about ten-years old who had real fair and tender skin who squalled like a baby and raised up after every whack. He was sentenced by a houseboy to ten whacks, but because he couldn't hold his mud his whacks were doubled to twenty, and when they were through with him and he took off bawling into the bathroom, his butt was a bloody mess. I mean when he pulled his pants down bloody skin was hanging off his backside like freshly ground hamburger, with blood running down his legs turning his white sox red as—blood. He sat on a toilet seat all night crying. Some of the boys teased him and called him a sissy and other names. And when the guard came in the next morning he sent the kid to the hospital but he didn't do anything to the houseboys who did it. They were in charge and therefore justified.

Another time I saw a guard make a kid eat his own vomit. In the mess hall for breakfast they often fed us a brown mush that tasted terrible, and the rule was that whatever you took on your plate you had to eat. So this kid ate some of it but couldn't finish it, so the guard, an old skinny redneck guard typical of the guards they hired for the low-paying jobs at the reformatory, he stood over the kid and made the kid finish eating his mush. But the kid ate a few more bites and then he vomited right in his plate, right in his mush.

Well the guard made him eat that too, mush, vomit and all, and nobody was allowed to leave the mess hall until his plate was clean.

And they made us take showers, too, which I'd never done before. They were all right, the showers, but I still preferred a good dip in the creek. Besides, I was twelve-years-old and just naturally clean.

My mother came to visit me once while I was there, her and Zeb. They brought me a half-gallon jug of molasses and a jar of peanut butter, which I had requested when she wrote me a letter and asked what she could bring. That's what most kids got from their people, those that had people, molasses and peanut butter, which they mixed together and ate till they dropped. Whatever was in molasses and peanut butter must have been what was missing from our diet. Me, I mixed mine together and ate till my belly ached and then I ate some more—and then I ate some more. Man it felt good. Unable to eat another bite, I shared the little that was left in my jug with my buddies when I got back to the dorm. Big hearted me.

There were black kids in Greendale too, but they lived in different dormitories and had their own chow hall and everything. I saw a bunch of them marching down the road to work one day. We had shoes, they didn't. So I guess we had it better than they did, but, still, I'd just as soon go barefooted as not.

One thing we had that was good was running water and bathrooms, which we didn't have in Hackney Land. And when I got back to the Land of Hackney I was aware of that shortcoming.

Zeb had never built an outhouse. And it was something that was never mentioned by anybody. He built a new barn for the animals. He built a smokehouse and a chicken house and in time a back porch and a front porch. But he never built an outhouse. And it was something you didn't talk about. Not that it made a lot of difference, we had a hundred and twenty acres of outhouse.

When I got back to Hackney Land I never ran away again, and since we had plenty to eat I never stole again since there was no need to. Greendale Reform School had slowed me down a bit. The only transgressions I committed for the next few years were of the domestic variety, like the time I was down in the woods thinking about Kathleen Vinson. Zeb Hackney caught me cold turkey with the evidence in my hand. He kicked my ass all the way back to the house and told my mother all about it in roundabout words while I stood there squirming with embarrassment. When he was done my mother gave me a stern warning not to teach my brother, Jackie, how to do That.

I felt like screaming at her that her precious son had been doing That ever since he was ten-years old, that you didn't have to teach a red-blooded American boy how to do That, especially if he had Baker blood in his veins. But I didn't say any of that, I just stood there struck by lightning with embarrassment that this strange woman who was my mother was talking about it in front of Zeb Hackney, God, and all of Creation.

Zeb brought a dog home one day, a little mongrel with short hair, white with brownish yellow spots. I don't know where he got it or why he brought it home but the minute I laid eyes on that dog I had a partner for life. I named him Lucky. He wasn't very big, maybe twenty pounds or so, but he wasn't no sissy. He could kill a coon all by himself, which was a job for a dog three times his size. And once he determined the boundaries of his territory he defended all that was within against all creatures big or small.

Me and that dog were close. I loved him and he loved me.

I remember one time out in the barnyard when Zeb was

kicking my ass, Lucky wasn't going to stand for that. He snarled and went after Zeb's big clodhoppers, all twenty pounds of him. So Zeb kicked his ass too.

However all things weren't bad for me in Hackney Land. I ran wild on those hundred and twenty acres and maybe another thousand on every side, exploring every hill and valley. I learned the name of every tree by both its bark and leaves, and I climbed them like a monkey all the way to the top. And I learned that if I climbed to the top of a slim young sapling I could grab ahold of the top and swing out and ride it all the way to the ground, bending it in half. Sometimes that worked and sometimes it didn't and I didn't have a parachute, so—it's a good thing I was made out of rubber.

And I learned the name of every bird that flew and when I learned how to make a slingshot out of a hickory fork and strips from an old inner-tube I shot rocks at birds until I accidently hit one, and when it hit the ground, dead as hell, I ran and picked it up and tried to revive it, took it to the creek and dunked it in the water; I did everything in my guilt to save it, but it was dead. From then on I didn't shoot at birds.

And Zeb didn't always cast a gray shadow. In the living room before a warm fireplace during the long winter evenings he sometimes soft-talked my mother into reading a book to us, for he couldn't read or write. He'd call her mama and butter her up and we'd all gather around the fireplace, me and Jackie and Zeb, three little kids, while she read the whole book out loud, every word, and during those times we were almost family.

Jackie, my tag-along little brother was growing up fast. When I turned sixteen he was thirteen, and already he looked a lot like Garnet Baker, our long-gone father. I had never seen my father in person but one day my mother showed me a picture of him, a picture she had kept hidden in a secret place all these years. In the picture he wore a sparkling white sailor's uniform, with a sailor's cap cocked at a jaunty angle on his head. He was a handsome man. My mother told me with misty eyes that he was the most charmingly handsome man she had ever seen, but he had left her pregnant with Jackie in the middle of the big depression, and she'd had no choice as soon as Jackie was born but to leave me with my grandmother and take off to Detroit with my newborn brother in her arms to find a job.

I had heard stories about my father from my aunts over in Dawson Springs, and from other people around town when I used to run away from home. Town was Princeton, Kentucky. Garnet Baker was the talk of the town when he was around, people said. Women would swoon at the sight of him just walking down the street. And if he stopped to look into a woman's eyes, her panties automatically fell to her ankles under their own power. I figured maybe that was exaggerating a little, but I got the point.

He was a boyishly handsome man with enough charm to melt the heart of any girl in town. He was also a blackguard, people said, and a drunk. When I met him in later years he was still charming and handsome, and still a blackguard and a drunk. But with all his charm and good looks women forgave him no matter what he did. He was staying with a woman in Chicago when I met him. She was a telephone operator, had a good steady job, which was a good thing, the job, because when Garnet was home from the sea, which he was most of the time—he shipped out as a worker on merchant ships sailing the Great Lakes—when he was home he spent most of his time in bars. When he ran out of money he ran a tab, and to pay the tab he wrote a bad check. But the bartenders knew him and let him run a tab and let him pay with a bad check simply because he was so handsome and charming—that and the fact that they knew with certainty that his old lady would be around once a month to pick up his bad checks and pay his tabs. She always did.

And while I was there this school girl, a young college girl, kept calling the house screaming threats at him for fathering her child under the false pretense that he was a lonely single merchant marine and captain of his own ship, so on and so forth, until he got her in bed sufficiently to knock her up and then he was gone. My father just laughed charmingly and said it wasn't so, and his wife believed him, for she had no other choice.

My father must have wrote hundreds of bad checks in his time on earth, but they say he never spent a day in jail for it because there was always a woman around to pay them off.

Well, at thirteen-years of age my brother looked just like him. But I guess he didn't inherit any of his bad genes, only his good ones. I got all the bad ones. Well, almost all; I never liked to drink much, that was the only bad one I didn't get stuck with.

And my brother grew up to be both handsome and charming. I didn't. I was a skinny gangling teenager with a homely face who became a skinny gangling adult with a homely face. And I had none of my father's charm.

But to show you how crazy things turn out in real life, my brother became a Baptist minister and used his good looks and charm to draw people into his church in increasing numbers. His sermons were presented in a compelling voice filled with deep conviction, not the kick-ass hell-fire ranting of many preachers in those days. And when his sermons ended, a disproportionate number of women, young and old, instead of dropping their drawers, as would have been their fate had it been Garnet Baker doing the talking, dropped to their knees and accepted Jesus Christ as their Savior.

When he was still going to school he courted and married one of the prettiest and smartest girls in the whole county, one of the Askew sisters, Mary. Or maybe she courted him, I don't know anything about that time in his life because I was in prison, but throughout life they stayed together and every time I got out of prison he had a bigger church and a bigger car and a bigger house.

And he liked to sing, man how he liked to sing. Every time I got out of prison and went to visit him we'd go over to his church and up into his hide-away, where he'd break out an old acoustic guitar and I'd play and he'd sing, mostly gospel songs, and we'd have a good old time.

And one night when I was playing guitar in a bar in Hopkinsville, him and Bobby Askew, Mary's brother, came down to the bar to hear me play. There was just me and a saxophone player and neither of us could sing, so once in a while we would invite somebody out of the audience to sing a song after they got drunk enough to sing. So for a while me and my partner played some saxophone music and then when the crowd started getting noisy we invited our first volunteer to sing a song.

He did, a country song of course because this was mostly a country bar, and when he was finished, with a lot of hooting from his buddies, another one stood up and then another.

All this time my brother, Jackie—well, now he was called R.D., Reverend R.D. Baker—all this time him and Bobby Askew were sitting there at a table sipping quietly on Coca Colas, but I saw the excitement in his, my brother's eyes, and the way he squirmed and leaned forward, and I knew without a doubt that he wanted to sing, so I invited him up. He pretended embarrassment at first but allowed himself to be coaxed and he took the microphone with a big "aw shucks" grin.

He had a good voice, my brother, and a lot of country charm. We knew a couple of country songs, me and him, and when he was through with them the crowd kept asking for more, so he allowed himself to be coaxed into singing another one and then another. My brother liked to sing so much that when he got started good it was hard to stop him, so when we ran out of country songs that we both knew, he asked if he could sing a gospel song, they were easy to play and sing, the old time gospel songs, so I said sure why not. The crowd was probably too drunk by now to know the difference anyway. So he sang a gospel song, and then another. And the crowd joined in singing right along with him. And the drunker they got the louder they sang, and my brother's strong voice soared above them all.

Once, while this was going on, the owner of the bar stuck his head in the door and listened for a minute, and then he told the bartender, a stereotype floozy blonde he was shacking up with in a trailer out back, he told her to tell me to stop playing religious songs in his bar. Which I didn't. I wouldn't have stopped if he'd held a shotgun to my head — not that I cared all that much about religion, but there was something going on here deeper than that. I touched my brother's soul that night. Or maybe my soul touched his, I don't know, but there was something going on.

It wasn't a battle between good and evil or anything like that, not a shoot-out between God and the devil, it was more like a search for something, like maybe the good and the bad curiously and cautiously discovering each other for the first time, like two dogs sniffing, maybe, or two souls groping in the dark feeling each other's presence but unable to see in the darkness, and then touching, the good and the bad, the first time touching, first the foot and then the ankle and the leg and the knee and then the sudden recognition of the missing half of each other, the good and the bad, two single strands of DNA that after all the feeling and searching discovered each other in the dark and suddenly embraced each other, wound around each other and made a perfect double-helix. My brother and me. The good and the bad. I touched my brother's soul that night. And I loved him.

I can't say he had the same experience. He was having too much fun. And I can't say it ever happened again.

Before I left the bar that night the owner fired me and the saxophone player, but neither of us gave a ding dong for it had been an old-time drunken revival meeting, if there is such a thing.

The Reverend R.D. Baker wound up as the pastor of maybe the biggest Baptist church in Chicago. I never saw it. I just heard from my mother what a grand church it was. And he, my brother, travelled to Jerusalem and wrote a book and populated half the earth with his kids and grandkids, most of them sturdy Christians, with some of them becoming missionaries and carrying the gospel deep into faraway lands.

And somewhere along the line the new Baker Clan disowned me.

I don't blame them for that. I never did anything to any of them but I guess my life of crime was an embarrassment to the family, and I accepted that. Besides, it never mattered one way or the other whether they disowned me or not, for you can't disown something you never owned to begin with. Jackie was my brother and the blood of our father ran through our veins, the good and the bad.

Anyway, shortly after I turned sixteen I had the urge to play a guitar. So a neighbor had an old flattop guitar broke all to pieces, but the neck was still good and it had three strings left on it, so I took a notion to make me a guitar out of that. The neighbor gave it to me, the guitar, and I took it home and hid it in the chicken house and during the day when Zeb went to work and my chores were finished I made me a guitar. How was I to know that the plywood I used to make the new body was the very expensive plywood Zeb Hackney was saving for something special that he intended to build out of it?

When I finished my guitar I hid in the chicken house and plucked on it till I halfway learned to play a few tunes on it. I must have lost track of time one day for I was still plucking on it when Zeb came home from work. He caught me, must have heard me when he came around the house to go in the back door. Well the chicken house door opened and there he was, looking straight at me. And that was the day he set me free.

He looked at that guitar, and then looked in the corner where his new plywood used to be leaning up against the wall and then his face started turning red and he looked at that guitar again and his face turned redder still. And then he said something and I said something and he snatched that guitar out of my hand and raised it over his head and said he ought to break it over my head and that pissed me off.

I came up off that stool with fire in my blood, the first time I had ever stood up to him, and I said, "No you won't." And I meant it. When I was sixteen I stood six-foot tall, I just wasn't very wide, but right then I was ready to fight and he must have seen it in my eyes. I thought for a minute he was going to brain me with that guitar. He was as mad as me. But I think he was surprised that I was standing there like that, and maybe that gave him time to think about what he was doing, for he suddenly turned around and went out the door without another word, carrying my guitar with him. He wasn't afraid of me, I knew that, so I knew that wasn't the end of it when he walked out the door.

And it wasn't. After a few minutes I stepped out the door myself. My mother was coming across the back yard toward me. She had a serious look on her face. Zeb was nowhere in sight.

When we met she told me Zeb had gone down to Doyle Hodge's and told her to tell me I'd better be gone when he got back, simple as that, I'd better be gone.

So I left. I remember the time very well. It was about three o'clock in the afternoon on an early Spring day, with about five hours of daylight left. And I was about thirteen miles from town and had no money or food or clothes when I left. And my mother didn't seem worried about that at all. I guess she knew I'd make it all right, that I'd find food and I'd sleep somewhere. There was nothing she could do about it anyway. She had simply accepted Zeb's order as law, and that's what it was in Hackney Land. If you were sixteen-years old and you stood up to Zeb Hackney you had to go. So my mother told me to write to her, and that's about all she said.

So I went. And she was already back in the house before I was out of sight. I know because I turned around to look.

Oh well. I turned back and went down the dirt road with a bounce in my step, the happiest sixteen-year-old boy in the world. Zeb Hackney had set me free.

CHAPTER SEVENTEEN

Something was in the air on Alcatraz Island that morning as we gathered on the yard for our morning smoke before work call. The sun came up just like it always did, and the sky was clear, with only a few white puffy clouds scattered like peacefully grazing sheep high above. And the water in the bay was calm. But the seagulls floating overhead were watchful, for something was in the air.

A brief puff of wind, just a breeze really, stirred up a dust devil that swirled away across the yard like a tiny whirlwind and died peacefully against the far wall. And the western sky far beyond the Golden Gate Bridge was empty of any threat of a coming storm. But the guard in the tower looked around uneasily, not alarmed, just uneasy.

Me, I saw all this and noted it in my mind, heightened awareness of things to come making me more observant of everything in my sight. I moseyed over to the bleachers and stood waiting, my thumbs tucked into my belt like a cowboy waiting for a showdown. It was a Zane Grey day.

I waited.

On the far end of the yard stood Roy Drake huddled with a couple of his buddies, talking it up, talking about me, pumping up their nuts, probably.

"See me on the yard in the morning." That's what Roy Drake

had hollered up to me from his cell the night before. "See me on the Yard." Which meant he'd worked up his courage enough to challenge me to a fight. I'd embarrassed him in front of his buddies in the mess hall the evening before, came down on him hard when I heard him bad-mouthing Jack Waites and Fat Duncan, for they were both in the hole again and therefore unable to defend themselves against such talk.

"You wouldn't say that if they were out here, asshole," I'd spoken up from the next table. I guess he didn't know I could hear him, because he turned around with a surprised look on his face and stared at me. "Yes, I was talking to you," I said. "You wouldn't say that to their face."

He finally found his tongue. "Hey, I wasn't talking to you — you got no business butting in my conversation." And he turned back around as if that was the end of it, and I guess I should have let it go, but I didn't. He had a couple of new buddies, guys who'd just come in, and he was trying to impress them or something, but he'd bad-mouthed the wrong people with me around, for Jack Waites and Fat Duncan were good people and I wasn't about to let their names be dragged in the dirt. So I said, "Roy Drake, you're a liar and a coward and you know it, and if you get up from that table I'll whip your ass right here in the mess hall right now." And I meant it.

"I'm not going to fight you in the mess hall right in front of the guards," he said, but he didn't have any baritone left in his voice, so I knew he wasn't going to do anything, for he *was* a liar and a coward.

But that night when we were locked down he had finally worked up enough courage to challenge me. He just had to save face, I guess. So, oh well.

I moseyed out to the middle of the yard and waited. He was still talking to his little rat-faced buddies. Maybe they were going to gang up on me. That didn't worry me a lot. The only thing that worried me was that I might grow old waiting. But then a prisoner named Jackolowski, who I barely knew, walked by me and gave me something to worry about. Without stopping he said, "Roy's got a knife." And he kept on walking.

Me, I didn't like knives and I never carried one or even had one stashed. A knife wasn't necessary in prison, especially not at Alcatraz where you were hardly ever out of sight of a guard, a knife was not necessary as long as you carried yourself right and didn't fool around with sissies or drugs and always paid your debts—and never ran your mouth to an idiot trying to impress his buddies, like I had.

Oh shit, Roy Drake had a knife and I had no tree to climb. What's more he, Roy Drake, was walking unhurriedly toward me now and he had one hand in his pocket. And his two little buddies were coming toward me too and they had spread out on each side of Drake and were moving faster than him, so it looked to me like they were going to jump me from the side before he got here, maybe hold me while he stabbed me. Oh shit.

I remember that day well and I'll admit I was scared shitless. I had underestimated a coward. I had broken a golden rule: Never threaten somebody—if you're going to do something do it, don't talk about it. I'd learned that from Al Doolin, but I guess I'd forgot it. And he'd told me never make somebody afraid of you, because a coward can be just as dangerous as anybody if he's afraid you're going to do something to him.

Oh well, here they came, cowardly Roy Drake and his little rat-faced new-buddies.

I noticed Jackrabbit over against the wall talking to Forest Tucker. No help there. Mild-mannered Jackrabbit was dangerous on the bridge table, but that's about all, and old Forest Tucker was almost womanly in his nervousness when it came to violence. I mean I liked the hell out of both of them, they just weren't hard-heads like me.

Little did I know.

The guard on the wall went back in his tower. Seagulls floated like vultures waiting for my death. Heightened awareness. Jackolowski walked past Jackrabbit and Forest Tucker, said something to them and kept on walking. I was aware of all of this, of everything that moved on that yard.

The shop foremen were gathered over by the gate shooting the bull. A lieutenant was with them. They weren't paying any attention to me. Where was Lieutenant Mitchell, Fat Mitchell? He was nowhere in sight. Maybe he wasn't working work-call today. I'd once seen Fat Mitchell jump all the way over the steam table in the mess hall one day to take a knife away from a black guy who was attacking Little Red—not Little Red Smith who worked in the glove shop, another little redheaded guy who worked in the bakery. They had put a black guy to work in the bakery for the first time in the history of Alcatraz, and the prisoners refused to eat the deserts prepared by the bakery as a result. Little Red had done a lot of talking. Well, during the evening meal this black guy waited at his table until Little Red came into the mess hall and lined up to get his tray and then he got up from his seat and walked up behind Little Red and stabbed him in the back. Before he could stab him again Fat Mitchell was over that steam table and on top of him in about two seconds, had that knife away from him just like that.

Most of the guards who worked at Alcatraz were a different breed from the guards who worked at other prisons. They carried themselves professionally, did their jobs, would not allow a prisoner to disrespect them in any way, nor did they disrespect the prisoners. And they were watchful, always clear-eyed watchful, for they had some bad boys to deal with. And deal with them they did. Me, I had nothing against a guard who did his job as long as he was professional about it and didn't go out of his way to mess with people. You knew what to expect from a professional. They did their jobs, nothing personal about it. Some of them I liked, like my boss in the glove shop, and Fat Mitchell and a few others. And I wouldn't mind at all to have a beer with any one of them if I ran into him on the streets. And I'll have to say that most of the guards who worked at Alcatraz were real men, though I don't know whether I'd want one of them to marry my sister or anything like that.

On the other hand, I'd rather she'd marry a prison guard than a sorry convict and become an Alcatraz widow.

But where was one of the sorry fuckers when you needed him? Not that I'd ever think of calling one of them, I wouldn't in a million years, but damn!

Another thing Al Doolin had told me. A stranger is more dangerous than somebody you know — because you know how to deal with somebody you know, a stranger you don't. I'd forgot about that too. Did Roy Drake's little new-buddies have knives too? They might be stone cold killers and they were coming my way — not in any hurry, just sort of easing their way in and out among convicts walking the yard, trying to act like they weren't intent on fencing me in; they were not even looking directly at me, just easing my way. Nor was Roy Drake in any hurry. He too was just easing his way along.

And that's a good thing for it gave me time to think. I'm not the fastest thinker in the world.

Heightened awareness.

The yard was full of factory workers, convicts getting in their morning smoke before we went down the hill. Convicts wandering aimlessly, grazing like cattle.

Grazing. It's funny I could think of that in the midst of danger, but I did. Maybe I'm over-dramatizing this in the re-telling of it, but I don't think so. I remember well how scared I was, and I was acutely aware of everything going down on that yard. Adrenalin was kicking my ass, the fight or flight thing. So, no, I'm not over-telling it. Every detail was permanently etched in my brain that day. I saw the seagulls overhead, I saw the sun coming up, I thought of Al Doolin and how stupid I was and all that. And I was scared.

But I remember that at some point I got pissed off at myself for thinking such cowardly thoughts. Was I a convict or a cowardly inmate? And that stiffened up my backbone. I needed a plan but couldn't think of one, so fuck it.

I was aware of Jackrabbit and Forest Tucker cutting across the yard.

I hitched my pants a little higher, took a deep breath and started walking, a cowboy with an empty holster, a cowboy without a plan, but still a cowboy. For it was a Zane Grey day, and I was walking straight toward old Roy Drake. All that was missing was some background music and maybe a tumbleweed or something. Fuck Roy Drake and his raggedy new buddies, too. Without a brain in my head I was on my way.

Jackrabbit cut in front of me, turned to face me and block my path. Forest Tucker stopped and faced the other way, toward Roy Drake, his back to Jackrabbit.

I had to pull up to keep from bumping into Jackrabbit. I tried to look over his shoulder, to keep my eyes on Drake. "Damn, Jackrabbit, what are you doing?"

He talked calmly, chest to chest with me and not moving. "You're going home next year—you don't need to be doing this."

"Hey, you two need to get out of the way, Roy Drake's got a knife!"

"We know it and we'll take care of it. Stay out of the way." Jackrabbit was talking like it wasn't nothing.

"There's two more, one on each side of him," I said, and I started around him, but he gripped my shoulder and held me still, gripped me with a hand of steel. "Damn, Jackrabbit," was all I could say, for I could not move.

"We'll take care of them, too," he said calmly, old mild-mannered Jackrabbit.

Well the two new-buddies had come up on each side by now, but they just milled around undecided, thrown off by what they saw, I guess.

And Forest Tucker was facing Roy Drake, who was approaching now. And Forest Tucker stood there calm as you please. Forest Tucker. I couldn't believe what I was seeing. He didn't say anything, just stood there.

Roy Drake stopped about five feet from Tucker, hesitated for a minute, then said, "This is between me and Bill Baker, you'd better get out of the way, Forest Tucker."

"He's going home next year. He's too short to be getting into trouble now," Tucker said, not a challenge or anything, just an easy-going statement.

Roy Drake decided Tucker wasn't a real threat, I guess, because he just sort of guffawed and stuck his chest out. "I've got a knife here, Forest Tucker, so you'd better get out of the way unless you want some of this, too," And he gripped the knife in his pocket with bravado, displaying the point of the knife through the cloth.

Well Forest Tucker spoke easy as you please, said, "I don't have a knife, Roy Drake, but we'll both use yours, if it comes down to it."

Forest Tucker. That's what came out of his mouth. It blew me away.

Well that threw old Roy Drake off. He looked at Tucker like he was crazy. He didn't know what to say. He looked over toward one of his new buddies and then the other, but they didn't seem to know what to do and turned away. Jackrabbit had turned to face Drake, now, and was shoulder to shoulder with Tucker.

"You too, huh Jackrabbit. I don't have a problem with you." He was whining now, took his hand out of his pocket, so he was through. But he was looking for a way to save face. His new buddies had disappeared, were nowhere in sight. He looked back at Jackrabbit, defeat in his eyes. But he had to say something. Jackrabbit just stood there, tall and straight, his eyes as cold as January. Man was I ever getting an education.

Finally Drake said to Jackrabbit, "This was just between me and him." He wanted to say more but he'd lost his nerve.

Jackrabbit said quietly, "I know it was between you and him, but you had a knife and he didn't, and you had two other guys to help you and he didn't, but he does now, so why don't you just go put that knife away and forget all about this and we'll forget it. And I do mean forget it, do you understand what I'm saying?"

Roy Drake thought about that for a very short time, decided he understood. He nodded his head and walked away. And that was the end of that.

But it was not the end of my memory of it and the education I got from it. Jackrabbit and Forest Tucker. Two old mild-mannered convicts, the baddest fuckers on the yard that morning.

They finally blew work call and we went to work, with me a lot wiser.

*****

CHAPTER EIGHTEEN

The dirty dogs tricked us. They finished the shack to house the new metal detector, then they installed the metal detector in the shack, and then they put out the word that the metal detector would be put into operation Monday morning. That was their plan, we thought. And we were ready to buck.

Benny Rayburn said it was just a metal detector that operated on magnetism and was completely harmless to human beings, but the convict who worked in the warehouse said just the contrary, that it was a fluoroscope and that it shot out rays that would make us all sterile, and that didn't sound good at all, the sterile part. To some of us, sterile meant you couldn't father a baby, to others it meant you couldn't do "it" at all—meaning you couldn't fuck, and that didn't go over too well.

So, whatever that metal detector was, we weren't taking any chances, we weren't going through the damn thing, period. We were all set to buck when we went to work that morning.

Well, we went down the hill to work and there wasn't no guard in the shack. It wasn't open. So we walked right around it and on down the hill wondering what was going on. And for the rest of that day and two or three more days, we went up and down the hill and nothing happened with that metal detector. It set there on the landing like a forgotten toy—forgotten being the key word here, for we got so used to it setting there that we forgot all about it, I guess. Then one day on the way up the hill to lunch, wham, they already had half the factory through that thing before we woke up, and then it was too late. They had tricked us good.

Me, I wasn't about to buck by myself, so I went through it too. I sort of believed Benny Rayburn anyway. But I sort of checked my Thing pretty regular to make sure it was still working all right, and it was, so I soon forgot all about that metal detector, whatever it was.

Christmas came and we got our Christmas bags and ate good and I hung a sock on a bar for Santa and it was empty the next morning as I knew it would be but I did it anyway for the memory of my grandma when my socks were always full, and then New Year's Eve came and Jackrabbit started a game of twenty-questions which we finished late in the night to the sound of tug boats bawing in the bay.

And the next morning it was nineteen-fifty-nine. My year to get out.

But I still had that detainer from Oregon for escaping from jail, so I didn't have much hope of going free, but there was still a chance. There are two ways to think about a detainer. The first is that you start pushing for a dismissal when you first get locked up—that way you settle it one way or the other, you either get it dropped or they take you back and try you for it and you lose, usually, but at least you know. The second way is you wait until you do most of your time hoping that as time passes the heat on your case cools enough so that you have a better chance of a dismissal. I chose the second way.

Benny Rayburn helped me write a letter to the prosecuting attorney in Portland, Oregon. It was a good letter, logical and clear as were all Benny's legal letters, not demanding, just politely requesting, for, as he told me, a letter to a prosecuting attorney asking for a dismissal of a detainer was not a writ, it was just a humble request—you've got to kiss a little ass, he said, because a prosecuting attorney was not compelled to do anything he didn't want to do. So I sent the letter off and waited for a reply.

January was a slow month. And, like most Januarys on Alcatraz Island, it was a damp cold month, and we hunched up in our jackets with our chins down on the way to work and back, for there was most often a wind blowing in from the west across the water and up that hill to greet us as went down and to speed us on as we went up. Even the slow walkers climbed those steps a little faster during the winter months.

Sometime during the month I got a birthday card from my mother. No big deal. She always sent me a card on Christmas and on my birthday. I liked Christmas but a birthday was just another day. Nevertheless the cards reminded me, as always, that somebody was out there.

And one day that month—I don't remember whether it was a work day or a weekend—one day that month of January I was puffing on a cigarette when Jackrabbit sidled up beside me and bumped me with his elbow. "Let's go over to the bleachers, he said," and he headed that way. So I followed.

Benny Rayburn was sitting there talking to Forest Tucker. As I approached they looked up and quit talking. Both of them had shit-eating grins on their faces, so I knew something was up but I didn't know what. When we were all in a bunch I looked around suspiciously. Jackrabbit was grinning too. As if on cue they all started singing like three idiots: "Happy birthday to you, happy birthday to you, happy birthday, Bill Baker, happy birthday to you!" And all the while they were singing I was squirming with embarrassment. I mean I nearly dropped dead. I was looking around to see if anybody else on the yard noticed what was going on. And to nail a final nail in my coffin a bunch of convicts who were hanging around here and there started clapping their hands and whistling and cheering when the song was over. Damn! It was awful.

Then Jackrabbit came out of his coat with a homemade birthday card which he presented to me. I took it. I could not do otherwise. On the front in big letters was HAPPY 23rd BIRTHDAY, and that really got me. I had to laugh, and laugh I did. Jackrabbit was on to me.

I opened the card. It was signed with a whole bunch of names, some that I didn't even know. Everybody was still grinning, and that's about when I started grinning too, I think. And feeling good.

They weren't through. Benny came out with a bag of goodies and we all sat around sucking on hard candy and shooting the shit. I guess birthdays weren't so bad after all— not when you had family and friends, and these raggedy Alcatraz convicts were both.

February came, and with it came the letter I'd been waiting for. It was a letter from a clerk in the prosecuting attorney's office. And it was good news. He said when the new prosecuting attorney came in he'd thrown out a lot of old cases and mine was one of those cases. I had no detainer on me now.

I still had a bunch of lost good-time, though, so I figured I might as well ask the warden to give it back. I probably wouldn't get it, but I had nothing to lose by asking. So I hit the wailing wall the next time old Promising Paul came down to the factory. I hated to beg, and I didn't, but I must have looked pretty pitiful just the same, for he took my name down and said he'd check on it.

And no more than a couple of days later I got a notice in the mail from him, old Promising Paul himself, that all my lost good-time was restored as of that day. And with that my new release date written in black and white right on that notice, was only two months away, the beginning of Summer. And the Hummingbird of Happiness flew up my nose.

Those two months went by slow but good. I counted every day, marking my calendar with joyful anticipation. I bumped into things, said stupid things, and forgot which end of a spoon you ate with in my happiness. And on weekends I walked the yard with my head in the clouds, grazing with the herd, wandering aimlessly here and there, this way and that. Short-time fever, that's what I had.

First order of business when I got out was a girl of course, but after that, money. I talked to Courtney Taylor every time I got a chance to make sure I had everything straight in my mind about counterfeiting payroll checks. Anybody could cash them, it was making them that was hard. And you had to have good ID. I stretched my brain all out of shape trying to remembering it all.

Second order of business when I got out was a girl, of course, but after that, money. I had to have money to get started with, to live on and buy check paper and other things I'd need before I could cash my first check, little things that I hadn't thought about until now, now that I was faced with the sudden reality of actually hitting the streets. Convicts build up fantasies in their heads when they walk the yard in prison, fantasies of big cars and beautiful women and tons of money, and I was no exception. We go to sleep in prison where everything is free, our food, our bed such as it is, everything such as it is but free. No responsibility, a bell for this, a bell for that, get up in the morning and do it all over again, the routine, the Rut—and you forget that on the streets you have to pay the rent. You forget.

Oh well, no big deal, just an inconvenience. I'd figure out a way. Maybe I'd borrow some money from a bank. That's where people got money from, wasn't it, they borrowed it from a bank. I wouldn't have any identification yet but I could show them my discharge papers from Alcatraz, that would probably be enough, wouldn't it? That and a thirty-eight Smith & Wesson revolver. Nope, just kidding.

I was getting out and I felt good, that's all that mattered.

So with my head in the clouds I finished those two months grazing with the herd. Forgive me but I like that word, "grazing," because that describes how so many of us did our time, wandering aimlessly, chomping grass here and there then moving on, grazing our pasture like contented cattle — or bored cattle, whatever, and now I was doing it, me. But I was a happy cow.

And it was while I was grazing with my head in outer space that I discovered the answer to the riddle of space and time. It was there all the time, so simple and elegant and logical. And one day I guess Mama Nature got tired of me stumbling around like an idiot looking for it, for she slapped me right in the face with it, smack, and suddenly I understood. And with the boldness of an idiot I present it to you, thus: THE FIRST LAW OF SPACETIME: *Space and time are equivalent, and neither space nor time can exist independent of the other.* I just thought I'd throw that in.

And on that joyful day I just had to share my great discovery with somebody. I spotted Benny Rayburn sitting in his favorite spot over on the bottom step of the bleachers so I grazed my way over there and shared it with him. About halfway through it he excused himself, saying he had to see a guy about a legal paper, and he took off. Oh well, I saw Forest Tucker and commenced to share it with him. He listened politely for a while but then his eyes blanked out. He finally reached over and felt my forehead with the palm of his hand. "You've got short-time fever," he said. And that really messed me up, so I looked around for somebody else. Jackrabbit was playing cards and Burgett was — gone.

I'd just have to bear my great burden alone.

And I remember that one day I was sitting up on the bleachers with Jackrabbit, just sitting and talking — well, not exactly talking out loud, but, you know, just sitting up there with our motors running but our mouths out of gear like you can do when you're with a good friend, so I guess you could say we were talking without saying anything. And like I said even when Jackrabbit was silent you knew that something was always going on up there in his head; he was on idle but his motor was always running.

Me, I was thinking I hadn't had a disciplinary report in over a year—yes, over a year. And that surprised me because I hadn't thought about it before. And I figured that was a big enough deal that I needed to say it out loud, to Jackrabbit. And I did. "I haven't had a write-up for over a year," I said out loud.

Well, Jackrabbit didn't say anything, so I figured he wasn't too impressed. But after a while, when I'd already forgot about the whole thing, he said, "I used to be like you in a lot of ways, but it's easier to do time if you don't fight it."

I nodded, waiting for him to go on, but that's all he said about it. So I put my mouth back in neutral.

And, I thought, I'd started taking naps. I hadn't thought about that either, until just then.

Fuck! I'd started taking naps! "I've started taking naps," I said with my mouth back in gear.

"You must be getting old," Jackrabbit said.

"I'm only twenty-three years old and I've started taking naps!"

Jackrabbit just chuckled.

I hadn't had a write-up in over a year and I'd started taking naps, surely a sign of something, I thought, alarmed. But Jackrabbit was right, it was easier doing time if you didn't fight it. Still, there was something about that that made me uneasy. But I was getting out so it didn't really matter, not then it didn't.

One day I got called up to an office where a man told me they were going to give me a train ticket back to Kentucky and then a bus ticket to Princeton, Kentucky, which was the nearest town to my official address and where my mother lived. I wasn't about to tell him I couldn't go back to Hackney Land so I said Okay, great and all that. A ticket was a ticket. And he had me sign some papers, my conditional release papers, and he explained that I'd have to report to a parole officer in Paducah by mail as soon as I got there. And I'd have to make monthly reports for the remainder of my statutory four-year sentence, which would amount to about a year—the length of my good-time. And I said yes sir, okay, and all that. And I signed some papers that said I'd do that.

And the shorter I got the higher my fever rose. And I felt so silly that I was almost afraid to talk for fear something silly would come out of my mouth, and also I figured my fellow convicts, with the loads of time they had left, didn't really want to be a part of my silliness. So I tried to be cool, to act like every day was just another day, ho hum, no big deal, and all that. But I guess my head must have been all lit up, flashing like a neon sign, and my body must have been giving off short-time vibrations—common symptoms of convicts afflicted with short-time fever—because everybody seemed to notice me and, to my surprise, many guys I didn't even know wished me well and seemed to want to share in my happiness, judging from their warm smiles as they shook my hand and talked to me about it on that last day. And, of course, Jackrabbit and Forest Tucker and Benny Rayburn were all over me making a big fuss, which I didn't mind at all.

And I didn't mind when Jackrabbit and Forest Tucker gave me a good old-fashioned lecture about how I should get a job and stay out when I got out, lectured me up one side and down the other, but I didn't mind.

I didn't even mind that always dangerous boat ride to the mainland, well, always dangerous to me because I do not like to be bounced around in a little old boat in the middle of a hurricane, well, not really a hurricane but, well, okay I do not like little boats in the middle of a big ocean of water even on a sunny day. But on that great day when I was released from Alcatraz, no problem. I was so happy that if that boat had sunk I could have just stepped right out and walked the rest of the way across that water without getting my feet wet.

I didn't even mind when a prison guard escorted me all the way to the train station, gave me my ticket and stayed right there with me until I got on the train, and he still stood outside the train until it left the station. They did not want any ex-Alcatraz prisoners hanging around in that part of the country.

Me, I didn't care one way or the other. When that train gathered speed across the Sacramento Valley on the way to the far mountains I was long gone.

The End

AFTERWORD

As I said in the beginning, I'm retired now. I'm eighty years old. Like an old car that's been garaged for fifty or sixty years I look pretty raggedy but my engine still runs. God lets convicts live longer. I suspect the Bureau of Prisons has something to do with that. The federal prison system and, especially private prison corporations, have high-powered lobbyists running up and down the halls of the U.S. Congress armed with millions of dollars in money and gifts to ensure that the tough drug laws that supply their prisons with endless lines of prisoners stay on the books, that the status quo is maintained. So if they'd go that far for their own job security might they not also lobby God for longer lives for their prisoners so they could do more time?

What happened between the time I left Alcatraz and now? You don't really want to know how to do hot checks so we'll skip that part, which doesn't leave much to talk about, but I'll throw in a few details to bring you up to date.

I ran into old Promising Paul up in Marion. The Federal Bureau of Prisons built the maximum security prison at Marion, Illinois to replace Alcatraz, but they closed Alcatraz before Marion was ready for new prisoners, so they transferred all the Alcatraz convicts to the four existing U.S. Penitentiaries: McNeil Island, Washington, Leavenworth, Kansas, Atlanta, Georgia, and Lewisburg, Pennsylvania. But by the time Marion was finished they discovered that the ex-Alcatraz prisoners had adjusted so well in the prisons where they had been transferred that they were no longer a problem.

The younger prisoners were the ones raising all the hell, the kids, so they sent them to Marion instead. I wasn't exactly a kid any more but I was just as dumb as one so they packed me up too on one of the first plane-loads of prisoners headed for Marion. That was my first plane ride ever and I was scared shitless, even more shitless than I'd been on that boat ride to Alcatraz. To make matters worse we rode on an old raggedy border patrol plane which flopped its wings to fly, or so it seemed to me. I swear it did, its wings flopped up and down like a bird and had big loose rivets that were ready to pop out at any second and plunge us all to an early death. That's before the Marshalls had a fleet of planes of their own. They often borrowed that old border patrol plane. I was greatly relieved when we landed and I was in a safe cell in the maximum security prison at Marion, Illinois.

Anyway while I was at Marion old Promising Paul came through there, just touring the place. Well he came into the print shop where I worked and saw me and I swear I thought for a minute he was going to hug me. I mean he really looked old and sad and when he saw me his eyes lit up. It may have been a nostalgia thing with him, for he was retired then. But we, me and him both, had a Bridge-Over-the-River-Kwai moment, and as crazy as it might sound, I believe if he had hugged me I might have hugged him right back.

And on another one of my trips back to prison—my new career wasn't doing all that well—I ran into Jackrabbit in Leavenworth. He was still working in the factory—Federal Prison Industries had factories everywhere, and still does. Now they call it Unicor and it's huge.

He wasn't playing bridge any more. There was a whole new breed of prisoners in Leavenworth by then, and they didn't play bridge. They played the game of spades, mostly, a simple game suited to most of the prisoners there, a game that lent itself to a lot of hollering and slamming of cards on the table. And you know Jackrabbit wasn't about to play a game like that. He was the same old Jackrabbit, quiet, easy-going—and underestimated by the chest-beating youngsters that walked the yard in Leavenworth. But Jackrabbit didn't mind that at all; he just sort of eased along in the background, as was his way.

He lived out his time working in the factory and was finally released. The last I heard of him he died of stomach cancer, that's what I heard. But he died free and didn't wind up buried on Peckerwood Hill. I was glad of that. He died free.

I, myself, worked in the prison factory at Leavenworth in the early years when they had the shoe factory there. I didn't last long. They had me working on a tack machine that tacked heels to the rest of the shoe. There were little holes in the heel and you had to put a tack in each hole, bap-bap-bap-bap-bap, like that—which was impossible. I missed the holes so bad that one day the supervisor came over and picked up a shoe I'd just finished and examined it, after which he held it out to me and in a loud trembling voice said, "Baker—when God created the shoe He put those holes in the heel for a purpose, that purpose being that each little tack goes in each little hole to attach the heel as an important step in the formation of the Shoe!" And he held the shoe up high for me to behold.

True story. Messed my head up. I decided I needed to find another occupation.

Leavenworth wasn't a bad place to do time in the seventies and early eighties, if you had to do time. All federal prisons were still under the influence of the Kennedy years and rehabilitation was the buzz word. But times were changing as people were beginning to realize that rehabilitation wasn't working. The same prisoners kept getting out and coming back, a revolving door of the same faces coming and going. I was one of those faces.

It wasn't that rehabilitation wasn't a grand idea, but it was doomed to failure from the start because the people who were responsible for carrying out the rehabilitation programs were the same people whose jobs depended on keeping the prisons filled up with prisoners, and who can blame them if their efforts were not whole-hearted. Their excuse was "You can lead a horse to water, but you can't make it drink."

The second reason rehabilitation was doomed to failure is that no one thought to ask the question: "How can you rehabilitate somebody who was never habilitated to begin with?"

So, to the relief of federal prison guards and staff the Bureau of Prisons gave up on the whole idea of rehabilitation. Their official policy became: "Our policy is to provide a safe and humane environment for prison inmates to serve their time." Meaning their new policy was to warehouse federal prisoners; rehabilitation was dead.

I ran into Forest Tucker, also in Leavenworth but in the early nineties. He was playing organ in the church. He was over eighty-years old then, I think, and he was in again for bank robbery. He sure did like to rob banks. He was playing organ in church, one of those big church organs that fill up the whole universe with sound. I went to church a few times just to see him play and he sure was a sight with flowing white hair and fingers that never missed a fly-spec on that sheet of music, and toes that kept up a steady "boop, boop" of bass notes to match. He played for the Catholic Church sometimes and for the Protestant Church other times, the religion didn't matter. And he played rock & roll music up in the band room with me and my raggedy rock & rollers. We really made some great noise up there.

That was in the nineties when Leavenworth was engaged in bloody gang battles. The gang bangers had arrived and federal prisons had not yet learned how to handle them. But Forest Tucker wasn't worried about any of that, all he wanted to do was play music and live to get out and rob another bank—or two or three. And at more than eighty-years old he still carried his own keyboard up three flights of stairs to the band room several times a week to play music with me. Man I loved that guy.

Forest Tucker was one of the most loved and respected

convicts in Leavenworth. He had carried himself well all those years from Alcatraz to Leavenworth and the older he got the more mellow he became. And when the nineties rolled around he had a grin that would turn stone into peanut butter. He was so beloved that the California Gang adopted him and invited him to eat at their tables in the mess hall, which he did, and which was almost unheard of because the California Gang was one of the deadliest gangs in Leavenworth and never allowed outsiders to sit at their tables.

Forest Tucker did his time and got out and the last I heard of him he was robbing banks down in Texas somewhere, old Forest Tucker.

And remember Courtney Taylor? Portly Courtney? The last I heard of him he was up in Wisconsin cashing war bonds, had him a big limousine and a chauffeur, the chauffeur being the kid he used to walk the yard with in Alcatraz, had a chauffeur's uniform and everything, the kid. They eventually got caught. That's how I heard about it, I read about his arrest in a magazine. He got caught, but he had a pretty good run, he did, which is about the best we can expect, have a good run.

Me, I was getting better at it with good runs of my own—trial and error, well mostly error because I learned from my mistakes but always seemed to run into a brand new mistake I hadn't counted on. And technology was moving so fast in America that every time I got out of prison I had to deal with brand new advances in crime prevention that Courtney Taylor had never dreamed about, like magnetic ink readers and direct telephone access to bank computers all hours of the day and night, things like that. So they didn't make things easy for me.

But, like I said, I sometimes lucked out and had some good runs. Once I stayed out long enough to get married to a wonderful girl right out of the nut house who believed in God and country and the pursuit of Elvis Pressley, and I'm not making fun of her when I say that. She was very special. She didn't smoke, didn't use drugs, didn't use profanity, didn't drink—she truly was a good person. She knew what I was doing to make my money, but she didn't comprehend it, and there's a difference. She was so naïve that she even believed the words of politicians, for she saw the good in everyone, even me. So, even though we had little in common, we fit together just right, the good and the bad. I even went to church with her sometimes and filled the collection box with a good chunk of my hard-earned hot check money and felt good about it.

And like I said I had a good run that lasted about four years. Then I got busted and my American Dream came crashing down.

After that I was in and out, out and in, had some good runs and some bad runs, but no more American dreams—it was all about the chase. Up and down the road we went: dumb and dumber, the cops and me, with them being dumb and me being dumber. But I was leaving them further behind, the cops, because I was getting better at my trade, but then, while I was looking in my rearview mirror I always seemed to forget to look ahead, and just when I started thinking I was Superman, smack, mistake number ninety-nine, back to prison I went.

I was working big oil company checks, Exxon, Shell Oil, Chevron, BP, all of them, and the big insurance companies— all payroll checks, no personal checks. And like I said I became the best there is but the best just wasn't good enough.

So now I'm retired, finished, done. I ran low on testosterone, I guess. And I'm as happy as an old steer grazing along in a never-ending pasture of green grass. I've got a girlfriend at the mall. I visit her every time I get out that way. She doesn't talk much, in fact she doesn't talk at all, she just stands there in the window of Victoria Secret's dressed in orange panties and never says a word. But I love her just the same.

And I've got a little efficiency apartment with a window I can open to smell the fresh air and look out at the little toy cars people are driving these days. They look like household appliances, the cars—there goes a refrigerator, there goes a microwave oven and a toaster and a washer pulling a drier, man, how funny they look, those little cars. And I remember the huge Buick Electra Two-Twenty-Five I owned back in the seventies, took a football field to turn around in and a city block to park.

I've still got buddies in Leavenworth that I keep in touch with who keep rooting for me to get laid, that's about all they think about, my responsibility to them and the whole world to get laid. But I try to tell them, hey I'm eighty-years old and Medicare doesn't cover Viagra so give me a break, but they still push me. Besides, I tell them, I live in a Metropolitan Housing Authority apartment house, an old folks home, filled up mainly with old women and they ain't paying any attention to me. They look good, some of them, but they ain't paying me no mind.

Well, one of my buddies in Leavenworth, an old black man who is deeply religious but not fanatical about it—for his God is all-powerful but not all-demanding—and whose advice I value most, he asked me if the old women were black or white, so I answered, uh, mostly black. So he said, "Look, pop"—he calls me pop—he said, "Look, pop, if you want to seduce an old black woman you've got to go to church." That's what he told me. And that leaves me out because my church is way out in the woods on a dead-end dirt path with no building and no preacher, just me and Mama Nature.

My church, which I discovered while wandering the trails of a huge park, is a special place where I go to tend to my soul. It is a place of quiet of solitude, a place among tall trees with birds chirping and bees buzzing and all that good stuff right out of *Reader's Digest*—and I'm okay with that now, too, Reader's Digest. I read one once in a while, the good and the bad thing again, I guess. My church is a place where space is equivalent to time and Mother Nature is equivalent to God. It's a place also where the good and the bad are equivalent, where neither the good nor the bad can exist independent of the other, for if it wasn't for the bad there wouldn't be any good.

They had a saying at Alcatraz that when you got off the boat on the way in you might as well give your soul to God because your ass belonged to the Warden. That saying is not correct. The Warden has to have it all, and when you surrender to the bells, as you must do, the warden owns both your ass and your soul. Forever. You can get out of prison but you can never be free, for the warden will keep the door open for your return.

But in my church in the woods I fooled everybody. I got my soul back. It wasn't easy. First I had to give up an exciting career of cashing hot checks. Which I did. Then came the hard part: I had to wrestle my soul away from the warden for he had been in possession of it for many years and did not want to give it up. But in the end after the battle of all time, he did. And now I have it, my soul, bruised and banged up as it is, it is mine and I take it deep into the woods, carrying it tenderly in my hands, and I lay it before Mother Nature, God, to heal.

I have a new warden now. From him I receive food stamps and I get an SSI check every month and I live in a low-rent subsidized apartment and I am insured by Medicare and Medicaid, so I'm all right for now. I say "for now" because I know my new warden will expect my soul before it's over. He already owns my ass, so it's just a matter of time.

But I've got news for him, I'm not about to give it up again, my soul. It took me too long to get it back. And I swear on a stack of bibles and my mother's honor that my new warden and all his men will not wrestle it away from me this time.

I mean I appreciate all that my new warden is doing for me. I am content and could easily graze along with the herd forever. This life is easy. The motto of the Metropolitan Housing Authority is "Grow old in place," meaning "Die in place." I am guaranteed to be taken care of all the way to my grave, all my needs, all I have to do is just give up my soul and take it easy. They even have their own Peckerwood Hill with a grave waiting just for me, compliments of the county, an indigent grave, an Unknown Convict grave, just take it easy and give up my soul, that's all I have to do.

Fuck that. They'll have to fight me for it this time.

If this book makes any money I'm coming up out of here. If it don't, I'll get me a guitar and rock and roll my way up out of here. Have you ever seen an eighty-year-old rock and roll guitar player? A pitiful sight, no doubt, but whatever it takes, I'm coming up out of here.

But first I have to heal my soul.

Deep in the woods near my church is a meadow and below the meadow a swamp: the flood waters of the small river that runs through the park. Seagulls often make their way this far inland looking for food. I watch them and remember the seagulls on Alcatraz Island. My meadow is overgrown with weeds, untended and left to grow naturally. And I remember my weeds at Alcatraz, my weeds that bloomed, whether it was a miracle or not.

And one day from my meadow of weeds I saw a seagull flying high, a lone seagull. And he was not following the river, he was headed straight west with wings flapping wide open. I mean he was moving out. He was a big bird, but no mistake he was a seagull and he was headed west flying high.

Maybe he was just headed to some garbage dump and in a hurry to get there, I don't know. But I think not. For in my imagination I saw him on the way all the way to Alcatraz Island, The Chosen One, going to free his flock. And at last those Alcatraz birds, who had waited patiently all these years for his coming, would fly away with him, free at last. And with the birds would fly the souls of all those convicts who had surrendered their souls to the warden. And they too would be free.

Just my imagination, of course, but still I watched that seagull flying high and headed west and my heart went with him. And I watched him till he was a tiny speck high in the sky, still headed west, and then he was long gone.

And then I only had one last thing to do, and I returned to my place in the woods, the bad looking for the good, hoping to find it there. But a voice told me I could not find it there, that I was but a single strand of DNA and I could not be complete until I found my other half in the heart and soul of a certain woman. And I cried "What certain woman? How will I know her?" And the voice told me, "You will know her when you find her." And that's all I was told.

So I went forth looking for that certain woman who I would know only when I found her, the bad looking for the good, and I wandered the streets near and far, for days and weeks and months I wandered. Would she have wings, or a halo? I did not know. And I wandered through the cold blowing winds of winter and the scorching hot days of summer, through rain and snow and—in despair, I wandered.

And then one day I returned to the apartment complex that was my home, weary and tired from my long day of wandering, and I found a chair in the computer room where I often went to work on my book. And a resident came in and sat at another computer, a woman, small, provocatively rounded and pretty, a woman I had noticed before when passing, a woman always busy zipping this way and that in a world I had not really noticed before. She was coming and going and she looked good both coming and going, but of course she didn't notice me disguised as I was as an old man, a forty-year old kid in the body of an eighty-year old man. I had done about half my life in prisons and jails and those years do not count when calculating age because when you are in prison you go to sleep and then you wake up when you get out to find that the world has passed you by.

The woman did not have wings or a halo but she did have a tiny candle in each of her dark questioning eyes that sparkled when she laughed and gave off an amazing amount of light when she looked at me.

Her name was Mae.

So, excited by my great discovery, I returned to my place in the woods to report my good fortune, and I cried, "I've found her, I've found her, at last I've found her!"

And I received no answer, only a chuckle.

So, puzzled, I asked, "What do I do now?"

And this time I received an answer: "That's your problem." And again that's all I was told.

To be continued, maybe, maybe not.

*****

RETURN TO ALCATRAZ, 2013

Yes, I was going back to Alcatraz. Me. I was going back as a visitor, a guest of the National Park Service. I was going back as an eighty-year-old ex-prisoner with a mission to spend the night in my old cell in C block, to confront my past, to confront that wild, twenty-three-year-old kid who occupied that cell fifty-four years ago and took me on such a crazy-wild ride. I was there to confront myself. That was the script.

That's the way the media was playing it: Ex-Alcatraz prisoner returns to Alcatraz to spend the night in his old cell. To seek closure.

Whatever. Me, I wasn't sure why I was going back, to tell the truth. I had just published a book, *Alcatraz 1259,* and I had sent it to Alcatraz to get it reviewed for approval to sell in the Alcatraz prison book store, and the Godfather finally got hold of it, the book, and, ka-blam, all kinds of shit happened. The Godfather didn't fool around. Like a streak of old-fashioned lightning, the book was magically approved, I suddenly received hundreds of phone calls and emails, and, wham, a thousand details were miraculously worked out at Superman speeds, and I was on my way.

The Godfather of Alcatraz, the site supervisor, the head park ranger, is Marcus Koenen, a soft-talking but decisive man of slight build and mild composure and calm but watchful eyes. He is a genius at getting things done without beating anybody over the head to do it. And everybody I spoke to, all the park rangers and volunteers, loved him for it. That's what I learned while I was out there.

But more about that later.

In order to visit Alcatraz Island you first have to visit San Francisco. And the park ranger who met me at the airport wanted to make sure I did just that. And, man, over the next few days what an education I got.

Her name was Wendy. She was a young "temporary" park ranger who explained that being a ranger was her dream job. She got the job after originally volunteering without pay to work on Alcatraz Island, where, after a year of proving herself, she was finally hired as a temporary park ranger.

Anyway, there was nothing uncertain about Wendy Solis in her little car darting in and out of traffic with the world by the tail, as she introduced me to the city of San Francisco.

And what a city it was. Right away it reminded me of the cities of many years past, Detroit, Cleveland, Kansas City, St. Louis, all the cities I had ever travelled through as I hitchhiked around the country fifty or sixty years ago as a runaway kid with bright lights in my eyes, cities that were once alive but now dead or dying. San Francisco was alive. It had a heartbeat. Everywhere we went, downtown or throughout the many diverse neighborhoods, crowds of people filled the sidewalks, going places and doing things. Thousands of small shops and restaurants were filled with people. San Francisco has no Walmarts. Walmart is banned in San Francisco!

The only problem with San Francisco is that the cost of living is almost double that of the decaying cities of the rest of the country. Even the cost of a hamburger at McDonald's is out of sight. Too bad you couldn't sleep in Detroit and wake up each morning in San Francisco.

I had a room in the San Remo Hotel on Mason Street, a short distance from pier 33 where I would catch the boat to Alcatraz. It was a single small room with no television, no telephone, and no bathroom. There were community bathrooms down the hall. Cost: $161.00 a night and lucky to get it. But, for all that, it was a really nice hotel, quaint, historic, clean, and the service was great, so I didn't complain.

My first evening in the city Wendy, temporary park ranger

Wendy, in full-dress park ranger uniform with a hat bigger than she was, picked me up in time to barely make it to the Alcatraz alumni reception at the Hyatt Regency, but no worry, she navigated the traffic like a NASCAR veteran and we made it okay.

The reception was awesome. Alcatraz Cruises, the official concessioner to Alcatraz Island, in partnership with the Hyatt Regency, presented a museum quality exhibit titled "Alcatraz: Life on the Rock" which filled a large chuck of the huge hotel atrium, an atrium that could just as easily have hosted a San Francisco Forty-niner football game, in my awesomely impressed opinion. I mean I just about fell over dead at the sight.

The food impressed me even more. With what seemed like an endless line of reporters hanging on my every word and every mouth-full of food I ate, I made countless trips to the serving table to replenish my supply of short ribs and meat loaf and mashed potatoes and salads and soups and some things I didn't know the names of but they were delicious.

I was a rock star.

Shucks, it's hard to be a rock star with both jaws full of food, but I did the best I could.

And I met some good people. I met Molly Blaisdale, of course, who organized the event for the Hyatt, the unsinkable Molly Blaisdale, herself. And I met Denise Rasmussen, the Director of Sales and Marketing for Alcatraz Cruises who impressed me a lot with her sharp wit and intelligent conversation. And of course I met Bob Luke, the only other ex-prisoner at the event, and several ex-guards. And, yes, I met Ms. Picavet, but more about her later.

From the moment I arrived I was bombarded with attention, which I loved a lot, but when somebody said I'd better go eat because they were going to take the food away promptly at seven o'clock, I promptly forgot everything I ever knew and headed for that chow line. Meaning no disrespect, but a rock star has to eat.

Sweet Wendy, with a hat bigger than she was, finally came to my rescue at 8:00 o'clock (they still hadn't taken the chow away and I was still eating, though I had slowed down considerably), so we found the Godfather, excused ourselves, and departed.

In my room at the hotel I crashed. During the night I had to get up to pee, as many old men do. I would have to put on all my clothes, walk down the hallway in search of the bathroom, *stagger* down the hallway. My room had a sink, a lone sink and mirror. So...the heck with it, I did what any red-blooded ex-Alcatraz convict would do in that situation, I pissed in the sink and went back to sleep.

The Boat Ride

The cruise boats are owned by Hornblower Corporation. Terry MacRae is the chairman and CEO of Hornblower. In other words, he's the man. They say he's on the move most of the time, flying here and there to oversee his empire, for his cruise boats not only carry close to six-thousand tourists a day to Alcatraz, but his New York cruise boats carry many more to the Statute of Liberty and Niagara Falls.

Luckily I met him twice during the weekend alumni event. And twice I was greatly impressed with his firm handshake and friendly manner. And even though I was the rock star on this trip I deferred humbly to his overpowering personality. It was easy to see why his companies had the concession to the three main attractions in America that could be reached by boat.

His boats were clean, modern and safe; his crews well-trained, friendly, definitely not like the raggedy boat I had ridden to Alcatraz as a prisoner many years before. It was one of his boats that I rode on my return trip to Alcatraz and on which I would leave before the weekend was over, for I had no intention of staying forever this time.

The weekend alumni get-together was a yearly event celebrated on Alcatraz Island by returning prisoners, of which there were only two—me and Robert Luke—and ex-prison guards and staff and relatives of guards and staff, of which there were many. The sleepover, also part of the event this year, was planned and supervised by Steve Mahoney, who had lived on the island as a kid. He was the son of Pat Mahoney, an ex-prison employee, who was also present. Steve Mahoney said, "The only bars I ever saw were the slats in my crib when I was a baby." Nevertheless he felt a strong connection to the prison and spent months in planning and preparing for the sleepover. There were thirty-five sleepovers, this year. I was the only ex-prisoner stupid enough to brave the austere conditions, the cold nights and lack of facilities. The cellblocks where we were to sleep had no heat, no working showers, steel bunks to sleep on, just like old times.

No big deal, I know I promised to take more showers when I got to be a dirty old man, but that didn't work out.

What did I feel when I first saw Alcatraz looming closer and closer? The script demanded that I *feel* something. I couldn't disappoint the media. What did I *feel*?

Nothing, really. I was busy sitting at a table bullshitting with Wendy and Ms. Picavet and others, while wondering about the possibility of selling my book in the Alcatraz Island book store, of making some money. That's what I felt. I had been broke ever since I got out of prison the last time and quit doing hot checks so I could write my book. Nothing else really mattered except the challenge of selling that book.

And it wasn't until the boat docked and we stood on land looking up the hill at the prison that memories came creeping back. But the boats arrive on the side of the island we never see as prisoners, except when we arrive and when we leave years later. So it wasn't a huge deal. The huge deal was those hundreds and hundreds of tourists coming and going up and down and all around like colorful ants. There was the long way to the top, the winding road with its many switchbacks, and then there was the short way, which was almost straight up by hundreds of stair steps. And the really huge deal was all those seagulls squawking up a storm, come to welcome my return.

But how did I feel, one of the press people asked me.

Strange, I replied, not knowing what else to say.

What I really felt was, man it's a long way to the top for an old man to climb, that's what I thought. But I bravely declined the offer to ride on the tram and I walked.

The Godfather

I had met the Godfather briefly at the Hyatt reception, but that scene was so crazy-mad, I hadn't really had a chance to talk to him, though I had received countless emails and telephone calls from him in preparation for my trip. Now I sat face to face with him in his office on Alcatraz Island.

First, to set the record straight, he had not bestowed the title of Godfather on himself. He was far too unassuming to do anything like that. We, I, had done that. In all my dealings with him prior to my journey to Alcatraz, he had cut through all the red tape in such a swift and decisive fashion, unlike every other government administrator I had ever dealt with, that it became obvious to me that he was an extraordinary man. He got things done. He got things done quietly and efficiently, but very quickly. Shazam, and it was done. Thus, the Godfather became his title.

Now many of his staff and fellow rangers call him that, *Godfather*, with affection, not deference. It has become a title spoken in fondness, friendship, comradery, you know what I mean. That's the Godfather.

His real name is Marcus Koenen. If I had to describe him in one word it would be "genuine." I say that because he turned out to be true to my preconceived conception of him after talking to him and dealing with him many times, but never meeting him face to face until the night of the reception. Seldom does a person live up to my perception of him in such situations. But Marcus Koenen was that rare exception.

As to how he had wound up at Alcatraz as the site

supervisor, he said: "I had been working as an ecologist for the park service since 2000, first in Washington DC and since 2005 here in San Francisco. My job in both places was to run a program that tracked long-term changes of ecological conditions in the parks. This included monitoring changes in vegetation or wildlife populations such as seals, coho salmon, spotted owls and more. My program also tracked changes in air quality, water quality, and climate. I really loved that job but was also starting to get more interested in applying how research results from programs like mine would get applied to making management decisions.

"My supervisor at the time gave me a chance to take a short-term position on Alcatraz. The job provided an amazing opportunity because of the complex challenges of balancing the monitoring of seabirds, preserving historic structures, all while providing a safe and rewarding experience for thousands of visitors each day. Oh, and I have to keep everything running smoothly with all the Alcatraz partners [the National Park Service, the Parks Conservancy (a non-profit organization) and the private Alcatraz Cruises operation] while keeping the professional staff highly motivated and engaged. Usually that means staying out of their way and helping out when help is needed. The challenges make my head spin every day and I love it. I guess I just like to stay busy."

Those are his words. Way to go, Godfather.

Why the concern? Because Alcatraz is and always has been battling the elements for its existence. A salty west wind blows constantly in from the sea and waves constantly crash into the rocks that form the foundation of the island. The historic structures, the cell-house, the walls, all the buildings, are crumbling into dust. The concrete and stone is turning to powder.

What do I care about a prison that kicked my ass black and blue fifty years ago? I don't know, I guess I'm crazy. But I do. I don't know why.

Anyway, I feel better knowing Alcatraz Island is now in the hands of another man who cares: Marcus Koenen, the Godfather of Alcatraz. History will remember his work.

The Ranger

Ranger John Cantwell first volunteered to work for the park service when he was just fourteen-years-old. That was more than twenty-five years ago. And he is still working, a permanent ranger, the ultimate ranger. Still as fresh-faced as a volunteer kid, he bounds up and down those energy-eating Alcatraz stair-steps like they are nothing. You have to be in good physical shape to be a ranger on Alcatraz Island. And he has been doing it for twenty-five years.

A dramatic example of what it takes to be the ultimate ranger on Alcatraz Island took place in 2007, when, just to prove he could do it, he, John Cantwell, swam from the dock of Alcatraz Island to San Francisco unaided by any fancy props or contraptions designed by man to protect a swimmer from the cruel fifty-degree temperature of the water or the dangerous currents of the bay. He simply pumped his nuts up like a young John Wayne and jumped into the water and swam to San Francisco. That's what he did.

They have a saying that the chance for survival in such a swim is fifty-fifty — that if you can make it from the island to shore in the fifty-degree water temperature in fifty minutes you might be okay, providing you are in good shape and providing the treacherous currents don't suck you right under and bash your head against a log or something, those currents created by two big rivers that empty into the San Francisco Bay and the tides that roll in and out from the sea. Never mind the sharks; they are the least of a swimmer's worries.

Ranger John could also talk, man how he could talk. It's a good thing most every word he spoke made good sense and was delivered with an easy-going clarity, because Ranger John could outtalk Buck Poe. But I could listen to Ranger John all day, while Buck Poe, even though he was a legend, made my ears hurt after a couple of hours. And Ranger John's boyish charm won me over from the very start.

He, Ranger John, was married and settled down when I met him that day on Alcatraz Island, but he told me he had a reputation in his younger years, that his nick-name at one time was Johnny Rotten. Nice girls were warned severely not to date him under any circumstances.

That he courted and married a nice girl, who was also a park ranger, is an Alcatraz legend in itself and a love story that would give the most hardened convict the sniffles. But this is not the place for that story and I only mention it to emphasize the unshakeable optimism of Ranger John. He was and is a remarkable human being.

It was my good fortune that it was he, Ranger John, that the Godfather turned me over to that Saturday afternoon on Alcatraz Island. I was to be the focus of a documentary video for the historical archives. John was the narrator, a job he handled as if he were born to it.

Filming took most of the day, with John feeding me questions with an easy manner that made my answers come naturally, for I am not a good talker, or at least I never thought so until that day. Now I can't get enough, for on that day, thanks to Ranger John, I became a super star. When a crowd of tourists gathered to see what was going on with the camera I talked to them, answered their questions easily, sometimes passionately. Because their questions were about prison life, and prison life is something I know about. And Ranger John was hollering at the camera man to get it all.

When the day was over I was exhausted but still pumped up on adrenalin. Man, what a crazy day.

We took a break, then. Ranger John took me to quiet area to relax and rest. I popped a chew of tobacco in my mouth and did just that.

Laura Sullivan of NPR News was coming over on the four-thirty boat to join me for the alumni sleepover. I would sleep in my old cell. She would sleep in the cell next to mine. Her

request to do that had been granted at the last minute thanks
to the quick intervention of, guess who, the Godfather.

The Reporter

I would sleep in my old cell. That was the news. What would
I *feel*? That would be the question, one of the questions among
hundreds more, as it turned out.

Laura Sullivan was an attractive blonde—no, I can't apply
that stereotype to her; she was an attractive woman who
happened to have blonde hair. It didn't take me long to find
out that she wasn't just any run-of-the-mill reporter. From the
minute I met her I knew she was different, that she was just as
crazy as me.

I'm a guitar player, maybe not a great one, but I still have
that Creative Thing that makes guitar players, all creative
people, crazy. And people with the Creative Thing recognize
it in others. Simple as that. Laura Sullivan possessed the
Creative Thing.

She had ordered my book, read it on the plane on the way
out from DC. Now she was armed with a long skinny
microphone cradled in the crook of her arm and aimed at me,
and that's the way she carried it the rest of the day and the
rest of the night and the following morning as well—except
when she let it down and pointed a camera at me, which she
often did.

She was a professional, a perfectionist. "Just one more time"
(trying to get the perfect picture) "Just one more..."
Apologetic laughter, she was really into it. And that was okay
with me. "Just one more, this one will be perfect." And then
another.

Laura Sullivan specialized in Crime and Punishment for
NPR radio. She had previously done interviews with
prisoners at the notorious San Quentin state prison, and
various other prisons and jails across the country. And when
she did an interview she didn't just talk and record, she had to
live the interview, to wallow in the mud in the bottom of the

ditch to feel the pain, to experience the life of the person or persons she was interviewing. It was in her eyes, her face, her every question. Laura Sullivan was a Reporter (capital "R" intentional).

I saw all this as the evening wore on.

Ms. Picavet, our stern but beloved chaperone, was the public affairs officer for Alcatraz. It was she who managed all contact with the media, she who made sure everything was done by the book, she who, with doting care, made sure I got plenty of rest and who refreshed me from time to time with water breaks and bathroom breaks and snack breaks whether I wanted them or not. If she could never become the godfather of Alcatraz for one reason or another, including the wrong genitalia, she certainly would qualify as the god-*mother* of Alcatraz. She was a wonderfully warm woman whose job it was to always say the right thing at the right time when dealing with all sorts of people, tourists, politicians, media, you name it, while maintaining her own sanity. She managed that all right, I think.

Anyway, she escorted us, Laura Sullivan and I, to the prison recreation yard, where we sat on the top steps of the concrete bleachers and looked out over the wall at the City of San Francisco, the Golden Gate Bridge, a scene I remembered well from the years I had been a prisoner there, except it's a lot prettier when you know you can leave anytime you want.

The west wind had picked up, as it usually does in the evening on Alcatraz Island. Laura Sullivan's blonde hair was blowing wildly. Nice. She asked Ms. Picavet to take some pictures of her interviewing me. Which she did. Seagulls squawked in the background.

Then we wandered down onto the yard, and ultimately to the fencerow where I had watered my weeds that bloomed, miracle or not, and the raggedy tree I had planted which didn't make it, thanks to a young prison guard with a mission, and at that point memories really came flooding back with a crash and I cussed old Simmons out right there on the spot, recorder rolling. I don't know what came over me, but I really got pissed off.

Forget that.

What was I thinking, what was I *feeling?* The Reporter wanted to know.

So she could feel it too?

We wandered through the dusty cell house, through the hole, D block, segregation. Ms. Picvet finally had to leave to join the other sleepovers up in the hospital. We were not deterred. The microphone was in my face and I was worn out, but loving it just the same.

What was I *feeling?* The Reporter wanted to know.

Finally it was that time. The time to retire to my old cell on the second range of C block where I had spent the majority of my time imprisoned. The time to confront my past, whatever. It was that time.

The question would come: What was I feeling. That's what my return to Alcatraz to sleep in my old cell was all about.

Laura Sullivan deserved an honest answer. She had worked for it, earned it. So we talked for another hour, microphone permanently implanted in the crook of her arm by now, and we took some pictures, "Just one more; this one will be perfect." Me and her were in my cell, camera set on automatic timer. And I answered her questions as honestly as I could. I was feeling strange, that's what I was feeling. I was feeling strong, as if that twenty-three-old kid was with me somehow, a part of me, that instead of confronting him, as I had planned, he had become part of me again and I was ready to rock and roll. I wished I had a tin cup so I could rake it against the bars about ten times to make a little noise for old times. To stir up a little shit.

I don't think I expressed that to Laura Sullivan in those exact words, because words come slowly to me, but that's what I was feeling. And I was feeling something else that I didn't say at all, couldn't say at all, not to her anyway.

I was thinking that the ultimate redemption of all time would be to seduce a woman right there in my old cell, that if I could do that it would be the Shawshank Redemption doubled and redoubled, the most awesome piece of ass imaginable. Just fantasy, I know, but that's what I was thinking that night, me and that wild kid who was inside me again.

The ultimate seduction in my old cell in Alcatraz—for Jackrabbit, for Forest Tucker, for Fat Duncan and Jack Waites, for Burgett and Benny Rayborn and Al Doolin and Buck Poe, and Punchy Bailey and Whitey Bulger and every prisoner who ever walked the yard in Alcatraz— and for all mankind.

And all the seagulls on Alcatraz Island would squall a mating call, and the wind would howl and lightning and thunder would flash and crash. And Alexandra Picavet, our sleeping chaperone, would sit straight up in her bed, suddenly wide awake, and know something was terribly wrong in her world.

And afterward I would cast a taller shadow on the land.

About one in the morning Laura Sullivan, the ultimate reporter, finally removed the implanted microphone from the crook of her arm and slipped into her sleeping bag in the cell next to mine. We were both tired. But I couldn't sleep. I could hear her moving around over there, tossing and turning, so I knew she was awake also.

For history. For all mankind. For Burgett who died out there in the Bay. A fitting celebration of life. Final closure on the island called Alcatraz.

The next morning, Sunday morning, the big day for the alumni event and I was dead—or at least I thought I was. Laura Sullivan was still alive, though, and back on the job, her microphone in place, a smile on her face, jaw set firmly, the Reporter at work again.

We visited the main book store (there are three book stores on Alcatraz Island), and I saw my raggedy book modestly displayed in a little corner of one of the many shelves in the big store. There were hundreds of other books, too, most of them written by the carpetbaggers, those authors who had never set foot on Alcatraz Island until they suddenly discovered that there was money to be made, and the gold-rush began. And like the carpetbaggers who invaded the South after the Civil War was over, they came in swarms to write books about Alcatraz, the Rock, whatever would make a buck.

The exception to the carpetbagger tag belongs to Michael Esslinger, Alcatraz Historian and author. He spent years in meticulous research and wrote a definitive history of Alcatraz prison that is worthy of being called a great work.

And I saw Jim Albright, an ex-prison guard at Alcatraz. He had the author's chair that day and was autographing books like crazy. He was wearing his old guard's uniform, which amazingly still fit him after all these years.

Laura had to go that morning, sadly, but she left me in the hands of hundreds of bright-eyed tourists, who had somehow learned that I was on the Island signing autographs and allowing pictures to be taken with anyone who wanted to point a camera my way. I was a rock star again. I gave speeches, took questions, what a day. It was like playing guitar for a large audience—give them love and they'll give it back a thousand-fold. And I loved every minute of it. John was with me, Ranger John, feeding me questions when it mattered, and the tourists were eating it up, me and Ranger John. Man, what a team we turned out to be.

And the Godfather was there, standing quietly on the sidelines, as was his way until needed. And Ms. Picavet, she was there too, watching over me like a mother hen, and somewhere in the crowd I spotted Terry MacRae, himself, the owner of Alcatraz Cruises, and Denise Rasmussen, his very capable Director of Sales and Marketing for the Alcatraz Cruises—and there was Wendy, sweet little Wendy with a heart bigger than her hat (she didn't have to wear her hat on the island), and inexhaustible Ranger Lori with her constantly flashing camera, and (who did I miss) more. Oh yes, I ran into

Chris Warren, the retail sales manager for the island, a quiet, mater-of-fact man who took care of the business of selling books and souvenirs on Alcatraz Island, and I met Elizabeth Siahaan, his boss, who worked for the Park Conservancy over on the mainland somewhere in a complicated partnership that I still haven't wrapped my head around completely. She was the "book buyer," a woman of few words but awesome results. She bought the books that appear on the shelves of the Alcatraz book stores. And I sensed from my brief encounter with her that she wasn't overly impressed by my rock star status. In other words, she wasn't a pushover. Oh well, business is business. While the Godfather and his crew of shining rangers ride white horses into the battle to save the world, somebody has to mind the store.

And I'm okay with all that. I mean, my raggedy book is just one of many that compete for space on the book store shelves, and I am just one of many squabbling authors who compete for time in the coveted author's chair to sign autographs and sell books—even though mine is the best...

Stop it Baker!

Okay, I'm done.

You've kissed about every ass in San Francisco. What now?

Shut up; I'm writing this raggedy story, and it ain't brown-nosing if you mean what you say.

Why am I dropping so many names? Simple, the names I mention are just as much a part of the story of Alcatraz as anybody else, including me and my sea gull buddies.

And not to forget Bob Luke, the other ex-prisoner who attended the event, he had returned to the island for the third time, he told me. He chose not to join the sleepovers this year, so I hardly got a chance to talk to him. But I learned a lot about him anyway—that he served some hard time at Alcatraz, five hard years, and, unlike me, that was enough for him. He was released in 1959 straight to the streets like me, but he got a job, got married and did all the right things for the rest of his life. He has a strong conviction that everyone has a choice on how to live his/her life, and if you wind up in prison, well, that's your choice too. End of conversation.

So, okay, back to the tourists—it is a fact that over half of all tourists who visit Alcatraz are not from America; they come from all over the world: Germany, England, Holland, Australia, everywhere. And hundreds were gathered around listening to me. It was daunting.

I was humbled by it all. I was amazed and humbled at the same time. And I think it was then that I understood.

This wasn't all about me. I was a part of it but it was bigger than that. This was about the legend of Alcatraz, the result of the hard work of the park conservancy and the rangers to preserve and maintain Alcatraz as it was in the distant past, and I was a part of that past. I was a living breathing Alcatraz convict, an endangered species very nearly extinct, and I was to be preserved and nurtured at all costs.

Ranger John had just a few days before scolded a tourist for unnecessarily chasing a seagull, one of those formerly nasty pestering seagulls who squawked noisily day and night and dropped their loads in mid-flight like bombers in a busy war. They were now protected, preserved, this was their home. In his speech on the dock to the arriving boat-loads of visitors, Ranger John speaks proudly of the seagulls: "And it is considered the highest honor if you are lucky enough to receive the badge of courage by being splattered with seagull poop while on Alcatraz Island," or words to that effect. And many tourists look skyward in hopes of being blessed by a direct hit of a lucky load.

And I was a part of all that, to be preserved and protected, a Gullie come home to roost.

And the tourists loved me.

Rejected all my life, at last I was home. And I was loved.

Maybe, just maybe, uh, if I could get away with it, maybe I could plant a tree out there in that fencerow on the yard. Maybe next year, on the eightieth-anniversary event. A tree that would live forever. Yep.

And it would be cherished, just like the seagulls and me. And neither old Simmons nor anybody else would be allowed to touch it, ever.

Yep, maybe that's what I'd do.

Snicker.

The End, maybe, maybe not.
*****

Tourists arriving and leaving Alcatraz Island. 5600 tourists visit Alcatraz every single day from mid-March through late October, 3700 every day during the winter season, and the tours are nearly always sold out. Of all the parks in the region, only Yosemite National Park receives more visitors per year than Alcatraz.

Super Ranger John Cantwell (aka Johnny Rotten) and me. In the year 2007, just to prove he could do it, Ranger John swam the dangerous waters of the San Francisco Bay from Alcatraz to San Francisco, just pumped his nuts up and jumped into the water and swam to San Francisco like it wasn't nothing.

Approaching Alcatraz—note the cell house high atop the hill. It's great to visit Alcatraz when you know you can leave anytime you want.

The Alcatraz recreation yard. See the concrete bleachers in the background where we used to sit high up and look out over the bay, and where the convict artists took their easels to paint freedom.

Jim Albright, ex-Alcatraz prison guard,
autographing books in the book store.
Amazingly, his uniform still fits after 51 years.

Interview with Laura Sullivan of NPR Radio, August 2013
"...for Jackrabbit and Forest Tucker and Burgett and all the old convicts, me and a gorgeous blonde in my old cell at Alcatraz — a fitting redemption."

Photo provided by NPR Radio

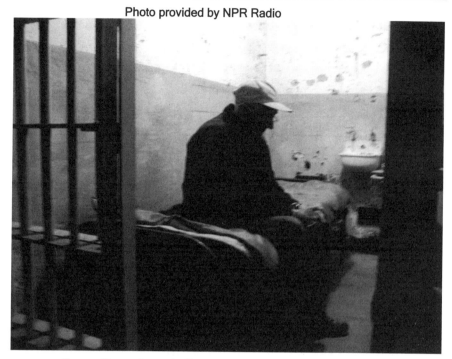

Spending the night in my old cell at Alcatraz.

Hamming it up with the tourists.   Photo by Devick Wiener

photo by Al Greening

Left to right, Marcus (the Godfather) Koenen, Ranger Wendy Solis (with a heart bigger than her hat), and Ranger John (Wayne?) Cantwell.

Celebrating the 79th year since Alcatraz prison first opened in 1934, ex-Alcatraz employees and families, (of which there are many), along with ex-prisoners and relatives, of which there are few, came together for this annual alumni event. They are the Alcatraz alumni.

(left to right) Ranger Carla, a rising star in the park ranger service, and Ranger Benny, a seasoned professional and all-around great guy.

And, yep, one of the old guard towers is still there.

Left to right, Marcus Koenen, Wendy Solis, Alex Picavet and Ranger Kelly Timmerman--and *food.*

Left to right: Bob Luke, the only other ex-Alcatraz convict who attended the event, and Terry MacRae, chairman and CEO of Alcatraz Cruises — at the Hyatt.

Left to right, John Hernan, age 92, the oldest surviving Alcatraz prison guard, and Steve Mahoney, who was born on the island, and who organized the Alcatraz sleepover.

Pat Mahoney, surviving prison boat captain (The Warden Johnson), and the ever-smiling Ranger Lori Brosnan.

As one of the last living Alcatraz convicts, I realize we will soon be extinct, leaving only the lowly seagulls to commemorate our passing, and I'm okay with that, for they are noble in their own way.

END